Judith Fiedler

Field Research

*A Manual for Logistics
and Management of
Scientific Studies in
Natural Settings*

Jossey-Bass Publishers

San Francisco • Washington • London • 1978

FIELD RESEARCH
A Manual for Logistics and Management of Scientific Studies in Natural Settings
by Judith Fiedler

Copyright © 1978 by: Jossey-Bass, Inc., Publishers
433 California Street
San Francisco, California 94104
&
Jossey-Bass Limited
28 Banner Street
London EC1Y 8QE

Library of Congress Catalogue Card Number LC 78-62562

International Standard Book Number ISBN 0-87589-381-3

Manufactured in the United States of America

JACKET DESIGN BY WILLI BAUM

FIRST EDITION

Code 7821

The Jossey–Bass
Social and Behavioral Science Series

◆◆◆ ◆◆ ◆◆ ◆◆ ◆◆ ◆◆ ◆◆ ◆◆ ◆◆ ◆◆ ◆◆ ◆◆ ◆◆ ◆◆

Special Advisor,
Methodology of Social and Behavioral Research
University of Chicago
Donald W. Fiske
University of Chicago

Preface

◆-◆◆-◆◆-◆◆-◆◆-◆◆-◆◆-◆◆-◆◆-◆◆-◆◆-◆◆-◆◆-◆◆-◆◆-◆

Field research is the design, planning, and management of scientific investigations in real-life settings. The work is done in alien surroundings: in hospitals, schools, factories, street corners, and homes. These environments are not necessarily hostile, but, unlike laboratories, they are not designed to meet research needs. Field investigators create the conditions under which valid research can be done. Using community structures and resources, the researcher must organize and control facilities and activities, either in person or through the selection, training, and direction of field staff members.

This book is a general introduction to field research. It

deals with logistics—the art of procuring, maintaining, and distributing materials and personnel. The book presents a practical methodology for the conduct of field studies, discusses techniques that facilitate fieldwork, and offers a rationale for determining the needs for and utilization of resources in the field.

Designing a working area, controlling work activities, allocating resources, and supervising staff members are management tasks. The skills that enable researchers to manage their projects are similar to those needed by officials in business and government agencies. Field research, however, differs in an essential aspect. In most cases, the research tasks impose on the ordinary activity of an organization or service, but the demands of the research cannot interfere with the basic purpose of the organization. The researcher who conducts field studies does so in an atmosphere of accommodation and compromise. To adapt to field conditions while maintaining the integrity of a research design is not simple.

If a field study is carefully planned, much of the effort will have been expended in planning, organizing, and arranging for the conduct of the research before it begins. By forethought and preparation, the environment of the field activities can be designed in such a way that the research fits naturally into its setting. The investigators' efforts are directed toward the end of disturbing the field as little as possible. It is an established principle of physics that the act of measurement distorts the process being measured; in everyday terms, when one inserts a thermometer into a beaker of water, the thermometer will cool the water as the water heats the mercury. Field research also will affect what it acts upon. The precautions that surround field projects are intended to insert the work unobtrusively into the real world. Studies that call only for observation meet this requirement more easily than do those that depend on some manipulation or interaction with subjects. The basic problem of field research is that of minimizing its impact while maintaining control of its progress.

Much of the difficulty can be obviated by planning. The

effect of an intrusion into the field is magnified by the speed and abruptness with which it occurs. Necessary alterations which are made slowly and cautiously can remain almost imperceptible. Application of these procedures in field research is through logistics. To a great extent, logistics can be expressed in economic terms. Maximizing gain while minimizing cost refers to exchanges of time, energy, and satisfaction, as well as money. In this book, the art of balancing resources and expenditures underlies the technical material.

Field research may be integral to the setting in which it occurs, or it may simply make use of a convenient location. A study such as the Hawthorne experiments is designed as part of the ongoing operation of at least some aspect of the setting in which it takes place. It is usually sponsored and supported by the management of the organization or place and is often viewed as contributing in some way to the productivity or satisfaction of the usual employees or clients of the setting. Many studies that take place in factories, military installations, or recreational facilities are of this type. The participants are asked to carry out activities that may differ from their usual practices but are directed toward similar ends. Experiments with changes in industrial practices and layouts, taste and convenience tests on food products in kitchens or restaurants, or the temporary provision and evaluation of special services to employees of large institutions are examples of field research that call for internal modification and study of an ongoing operation.

The location of other studies, however, might be the result of a purely adventitious decision. The choice of research setting may depend on no more than finding a combination of high occupancy and an agreeable theater manager who permits interviewers to survey moviegoers as they wait in the lobby for the feature film to begin, or a public school superintendent who can be convinced that observation of fourth-grade gym classes will do no harm to the children and will be of service to an old friend who now does research for a shoe manufacturer.

The field researcher may work as an independent individual, but it is more common for field studies to be conducted under the egis of some parent organization that offers certification and legitimacy. When the locus of the study is an organization or agency within the community, institutional sponsorship permits the investigator to interact with people and organizations on an equal footing. Studies that occur under the auspices of an organization usually benefit from this relationship, since the investigator will have access to facilities and support from the administration.

Even a memo from the general manager recommending cooperation or the assignment of a junior officer to act as liaison for the study, however, will not relieve the researcher from the necessity of deciding what must be provided and how it is to be used. He or she may no longer have the personal duty of checking the tape recorder and measuring the stage, but solving the problems of a machine that does not work or a platform that is too small remains the responsibility of the investigator.

Most people remember the ambiguities and anxieties of the first days on a new job. Learning the required and forbidden behaviors and the unwritten rules comes slowly, so that it may be some time before the new staff member knows which door is the right one for a person of his rank to use, or how long he must wait before bringing in his own potted plants or removing the prior occupant's pictures without giving offense. Violating these norms may have no direct consequences but can set up barriers between the individual and the smooth operation of the organization's system. In many senses, fieldwork replicates such entry situations over and over. Each project requires the adaptive process to a new setting, with all its attendant stresses and uncertainties, and experience in one situation may only minimally carry over to the next. The researcher must step into this world cautiously. The costs of error are high, not only in personal uneasiness but in the damage that might be done to the impartiality and replicability of the work.

There is no way to eliminate these problems altogether, but advance preparation can minimize them. The disruption caused by poor organization should not be added to the inevitable confusions associated with doing unusual things in strange places. Instead, every solution and adaptation that can be managed beforehand contributes to the participants' impression of the investigator's assurance and control. In turn, their ease and comfort in the experimental process depends on their conviction that the investigator knows what is about to happen and is prepared for it. At times, of course, the research demands that certain stresses be placed on its participants, but these must be controlled stresses. It may be necessary for the subjects to feel anxious about the results of an experimental conflict, but there is no excuse for imposing on them anxiety over whether the experimenters themselves know what is going on.

Disorganization and recurrent crises do more harm than simply demanding attention that must be subtracted from research activities. By modifying the conditions under which the work is done, they create new and unanticipated variables which cannot be accounted for in the analyses of the data.

In one way or another, most research involves the measurement of a subject's response to stimuli. Controlling the intensity and type of stimulus is easy under laboratory conditions. Equipment can be constructed to deliver precisely calibrated levels of scent or light; sophisticated electronic devices can give access to or abruptly cut off communications or switch patterns of interaction from one system to another; adequate light for the cameras will be available, and furniture can be bolted into position to manipulate the spacing and movements that the design calls for. In the field, the environment is less amenable to control.

The research reports that reach publication rarely address such issues in detail. Questions of space, supplies, and personnel management do not bear directly on the elegance of a research design or the statistical validity of its results. Failure to solve these practical problems, however, can negate the most polished plan and can permit contamination, which seriously threatens validity. The logistics of field research deal with trivial details that are not trivial in their effects.

The practitioners of field research include university-

Preface

based faculty and students in the social and health sciences; planners and evaluators of public programs and services; and people in market research, advertising, and politics. Many of them have had university training in research methodology and are sophisticated in statistical analysis and research design. Others have learned on the job, gradually developing expertise in identifying and defining appropriate areas for investigation. Neither college courses in methodology nor standard texts on research design devote much time to the practical issues of what to do when. Moving from the classroom to real research with real people can be a painful and costly experience.

Field Research is planned to fit into this gap between theory and practice. As a supplementary text for college methodology courses, it can provide the student with a realistic account of field problems and solutions, fleshing out the scanty references in other sources. For graduate students engaging in thesis or dissertation field projects, it can serve as a handbook for design and management. And for urban planners, public utility researchers, marketing demand specialists, and service program evaluators, it can simplify and thus facilitate applied investigations.

The chapters in this book deal with various aspects of field research management, in roughly the order that each subject will be considered by the researcher in planning and carrying out a field study. Field projects, however, rarely operate in a straight line. Elements of each of the stages are interrelated throughout the period of the research, as events and the modifications they occasion affect the work. The reader, searching here for assistance in conducting a field study, will find it useful to read through the book, tracing the progress of the various aspects as they interact, before returning to look more critically at each subject.

Acknowledgments

Field Research is based on many years of field experience. I am deeply grateful to the many subjects and participants who

Preface

allowed me to work with them in conducting these studies, and in the process, taught me how to manage fieldwork. I also wish to thank Brenda Goldstein, whose skilled work prepared this manuscript for the publisher. For its content, I owe thanks to Robert Ferber and Seymour Sudman at the Survey Research Laboratory of the University of Illinois at Urbana-Champaign, where I learned my trade; to Clifford E. Lunneborg at the Educational Assessment Center of the University of Washington, who encouraged me to practice it; and to my husband, Fred E. Fiedler, who stood by.

Seattle, Washington   Judith Fiedler
August 1978

Contents

◆◆◆◆◆◆◆◆◆◆◆◆◆◆◆◆◆◆◆◆◆◆◆◆◆◆◆◆◆◆◆◆◆

xv

Contents

The Author

◆◆◆◆◆◆◆◆◆◆◆◆◆◆◆◆◆◆◆◆◆◆◆◆◆◆◆◆◆◆◆◆◆◆◆

Judith Fiedler is assistant director of the University of Washington's Educational Assessment Center where she has been since 1969. Her primary responsibility is the design and conduct of field studies for university, government, and public service agencies and the direction of university programs of evaluative survey research. As consultant to government and private evaluation and planning organizations, she has designed and directed numerous field studies of service delivery systems, and she presently serves on local government committees on community planning and citizen participation in government.

Fiedler received the bachelor's degree from the University

The Author

of Chicago and, in 1972, the master's degree in sociology from the University of Washington. She has published journal articles on survey research and is the author of technical reports, field staff training, and procedural manuals. From 1967 to 1969, she directed fieldwork for the Survey Research Laboratory of the University of Illinois and, in 1973, for Battelle Human Affairs Research Centers.

Field Research

A Manual for Logistics and Management of Scientific Studies in Natural Settings

One

Planning for Field Operations

❖◆❖◆◆❖◆❖◆❖◆❖◆❖◆❖◆❖◆❖◆❖◆❖◆❖◆❖◆❖◆❖◆

You have elaborated the hypotheses, reviewed the literature, and determined the appropriate statistical strategies for the research problem. All that remains is to conduct the study. The data may be collected in libraries or laboratory experiments. Your particular project, however, requires you to work in a setting that has a real-life existence, one not specifically designed for the purposes of research. In such studies, the subjects are not college students earning course credit or a token payment; they are participants by virtue of their membership in some community or institution in which the research is done. They may be housewives exercising at a city park, employees in an office or factory, or ticket buyers at a sporting event. The research tasks they are

1

asked to undertake may have little relevance to their ordinary lives and are likely to interrupt or impede their usual activities. In some cases, the interruption may be pleasant for the participants. An Army platoon, for example, may be detached from regular training duties and formed into committees to solve puzzles as a study of communication channels, or shoppers at a supermarket may be asked to taste food samples or rate advertising presentations. Under other conditions, the research may well be seen as an unwelcome task imposed by higher authority; for example, experimental changes may be made in work procedures, or individuals may be asked to perform actions that are unimportant or of no interest to them. You must obtain their willing cooperation, as well as formal authorization to enlist their aid. But even before work with the subjects begins, the setting and conditions under which the research will take place must be established. Defining and locating the appropriate research sites, specifying the procedures to be followed, and finding and securing the supplies and equipment that are required are the preconditions for successful fieldwork. Sufficient time, money, and skill must be allocated to meeting each of these requirements.

Field studies usually require a team of researchers—either staff members of a parent organization who are experienced in the type of study conducted or people, whether trained or untrained, who are hired or volunteer for a particular project. No matter how often a group of staff members have worked together, each study demands some special training for its unique elements. A field staff must be recruited, trained, and supervised; and, again, sufficient resources must be set aside for these tasks. An individual can, of course, conduct field research alone. The effort of a single researcher planning, organizing, and carrying out field procedures is typical of studies by students working toward advanced degrees, but it is not limited to students. Individuals, however, are less likely to have adequate resources than are organizations and institutions. If you intend to undertake a field study by yourself, extra forethought is essential.

Planning for Field Operations

Working alone does not decrease the need for planning—particularly in scheduling and the efficient use of time. A single researcher cannot be in two places at the same time and can work only a limited number of hours in a day. One person interviewing for six hours cannot quite manage the burden that three people can carry for two hours each. As an independent researcher, you can expect the demands on your resources and energy to be great. They should not be underestimated.

After gathering the necessary resources and arranging for their deployment, you must also plan how they are to be used, allowing sufficient time for the tasks but minimizing waste in time and materials. If you are working with the support of an organization, it is probably unnecessary to remind you that money should be used carefully. Simple courtesy also dictates that you be equally thrifty with human resources. You are responsible for the efficient use of the subjects' time, as well as your own.

Finally, field research calls for things in the right places: data collection instruments, items to be evaluated, measuring devices, office supplies, and the records in which the work will be described and documented. These supplies must be designed, purchased, or made and must be at hand when they are needed.

Controlling all these factors requires exact answers to questions of what should be done, what is being done, what material and human resources are needed, and how they are to be used. Even the simplest research project must answer these questions in a way that not only facilitates the work but maintains a record of the materials and procedures used. Unfortunately, this information is rarely reported, even in the most carefully written research publications.

A typical excerpt from the procedural description of a field research project[1] states: "Interviews were held with parents of prospective subjects in their homes and with the minis-

[1] M. Sherif and C. W. Sherif, *Groups in Harmony and Tension: The Robbers' Cave Experiment* (New York: Harper & Row, 1953).

ters of their church groups. Information sheets were filled in. Before the experiment several tests were administered" (p. 238). "This study . . . was conducted at an isolated camp site" (p. 240). Only gradually do later references to the specifications of buildings, athletic fields, "junior counselors," seating charts, records of incoming and outgoing mail, watermelons, chocolate bars, and other desirable tokens suggest what requirements had to be met. A statement such as "The adult staff members had at hand the essential equipment . . . tents, canteens, food, equipment, and so on" (p. 243) signals that certain procurement activities must have occurred but does not explain how. Another statement describes the appearance of the ice cream and cake used in the experiment: "Half of them had been battered, broken, or crushed to appear as though something had happened to them in transit; the other half remained whole and delectable" (p. 278). All this information should alert the investigator to a number of questions: Under what conditions were the interviews conducted? By whom? Who provided the information sheets, test forms, seating charts, and mail tallies which are mentioned? Who selected, bought, and delivered the athletic and camping equipment, and where was it stored until use? And, most intriguing, how were the refreshments damaged according to specification?

The previous quotations and those that follow are taken from monographs, rather than from articles in technical or research journals. Under the more stringent space restrictions for journals, even less information is given. Journal articles usually do not spell out exactly how the procedures were carried out and what adaptations or corrections had to be made in the original plans. At best, such information may be retained in working papers or field notes. Most often, it exists only in the researcher's memory. Fortunately, in a later report[2] on the study cited in the preceding paragraph, many of the field details are de-

[2] M. Sherif and others, *Intergroup Conflict and Cooperation* (Norman: Institute for Group Relations, University of Oklahoma, 1954).

4

scribed. For instance, this later report addresses the issue of subject selection, which "required a city of sufficient size to have enough schools so only one boy could be selected from each school. The city was divided into three areas. Each was assigned to the one of the three interviewers who knew best that particular section. The principals of the appropriate schools were contacted" (p. 65). "The site was finally chosen after inspection of a number of camps. Effective isolation was made possible by a surrounding fence with 'Keep Out' and 'Restricted' signs" (p. 66). Even in this expanded description, however, some points of curiosity remain. The experiment required, for example, that the investigators interfere with the camp's supply of drinking water by stuffing a cloth into a water outlet. Obviously, concern for the boys' health required that the cloth be very clean and preferably sterile. Sterilizing the cloth and protecting it until its insertion into the tank, then, was still another field task. At a later point in the study, the boys were led to cooperate on moving a stalled truck. The truck itself was part of the camp's equipment and was usually in good working order. A mechanically inclined researcher probably could disable it temporarily, but someone would have to make sure that a researcher with the proper mechanical skills, and any necessary tools, was on duty at that time and place.

Managing such details is precisely what you, as director of a field project, must undertake. The tasks are specified in the research design, at least in general terms. But each major step breaks down into a number of subtasks, which you may not recognize until you are already engaged in the process. Each of the subtasks must be described and scheduled in turn, and any of them may become still other and more complex involutions of the original activity. The tasks and subtasks must be operationally defined and assigned to people who are capable of completing them. These people must be equipped with the supplies they need; they must also be provided with a place where they can do their work. In order to make reasonable arrangements for providing and managing people, places, and things, you will

5

need some method for organizing and presenting the practical problems of field research and spelling out the requirements for solving them. An effective method is the development of an operations schedule.

The Operations Schedule

An operations schedule is simply a list of the tasks to be performed and a record of the conditions that must be met to allow successful performance. The operations schedule may be no more than a note written to yourself, reminding you to pick up extra tapes before setting out to record an interview. Even this task, however, will be easier if the note also mentions what kind of tape cassette is needed, what store has a supply at the lowest price, and when the purchase should be made (for instance, before you leave the office for lunch or after you have cashed an expense voucher at the purchasing desk). Even more information is needed if the task is given to someone else or interspersed with other activities. Under these conditions, detailed instructions (Cash voucher at Purchase Desk—closed between 12:00 and 1:00. Buy ten Maxell ninety-minute tapes at City Office Supply—should get special price of 10 percent off on box. Pack them with the cue cards—ready at Printing Room —with the supplies we'll take on the 3:40 bus) will assure that anyone given the job will be able to complete it satisfactorily. An operations schedule provides this information. It also identifies the target dates—the times when actions must be completed if the study is to meet its goal. Operational instructions for the task can be presented as shown in Figure 1.

How important is it that the schedule be written in such detail? It is not important at all if the researcher alone performs simple tasks, has an excellent memory, and can be absolutely certain that nothing will go wrong with his or her arrangements. A schedule also may not be important if the study can be interrupted or rescheduled almost at will—for instance, if the researcher merely has to observe some continuing process or

Planning for Field Operations

Figure 1. Basic Operations Schedule

What must be done? (Task)	Where will it be done? (Location)	Who does it?* (Staff)	What materials are needed for the task? (Materials)	When must it be done? (Time)
1. Cash in voucher	Purchase office	Sally	Signed voucher I.D. card	Before 12:00 or between 1:00 and 2:00 (allow time for shopping)
2. Buy tapes	City Office Supply, 1601 Madison	Sally	Order blank Cash	Before 2:30 (allow time to pack supply box)
3. Pick up cue cards	Printing room	Ben	Requisition	Before 2:45 (allow time to pack supply box)
4. Pack supply box	Workroom	Ben	Supply list, box, tape, cord, labels	Before 3:00 (must leave for bus station by 3:15)
5. Get supplies to bus	Greyhound terminal, 8th and Stewart door, freight office	LKM or Ben	Address labels for box, cash for prepayment Car or truck	Before 3:40 (bus leaves on time!)

*Assign the job to only one person, and make sure that he or she is aware of the responsibility.

follow a procedure not affected by its surroundings. It may make very little difference whether one watches passengers descending from an elevated train on a Tuesday or a Wednesday or hands out brochures this week or next.

When, however, elements of the study depend on the characteristics of the setting or population, and when researchers must interact with subjects, the researchers must be able to control and predict what will happen. Under these conditions, the schedule should be written, so that the plans will be clear to the researcher and others and so that documentation of the project will be available at a later time. The basic schedule for a relatively simple field research project would be brief.

Field Research

For example, some graduate students wanted to study the purchasing behavior of visitors to a sidewalk arts and crafts fair as a test of the hypothesis that social relations with vendors are positively related to favorable evaluation of products. The study would attempt to relate actual purchase of goods with the personal and social interactions among shoppers and artists. The data would be collected by observation, and the artists had to agree to align their booths so that physical access would be equal to each. At a meeting of the research team, the plans for the fieldwork were discussed:

"All right, now we've decided which behaviors we're going to score. We can just tally them on sheets of paper."

"We should make up a sort of score sheet, though, so it will be easier to add them up at the end."

"What else do we have to do?"

"Remember, we have to get clearance from the Human Subjects Committee."

"Have we got a place to observe from?"

"The bookstore office is on the second floor. Maybe they'll let us use their windows."

"Until 9:00 at night?"

"I didn't know we were going to work all evening."

"Sure, the fair is going on until 9:00."

"The bookstore closes at 6:00."

"That means making up a time schedule, so we'll be sure someone is always there."

"Will they let anybody just come in, or should we get a key?"

"I'm not sure we'll be low enough to see the booths. They'll have to be set back far enough so we can see the sidewalk in front."

8

Planning for Field Operations

"Somebody's going to have to get there before the fair opens, to make sure things are set up properly, on both days."

At some point during this discussion, an efficient researcher would begin to set things down on paper. Developing an operations schedule is the essential first step in management activities. It starts as a single sheet, specifying the tasks, defining the subtasks, and identifying the points on the time schedule during which this work should take place. The tasks vary according to the research design, but they must at least include provisions for a suitable place where the research will occur, people to carry out the work, and necessary supplies and materials. The actions should be listed chronologically, with clear indications of dependent factors—that is, which actions must be completed *before* a subsequent activity can take place—and the cutoff times by which certain steps must be completed.

The primary task of the team in the example was simply that of observation and recording. In order to carry out this task, they needed access to a place from which observations could be made, a way of standardizing the units that were to be the targets of behavior, a system of work assignments, and materials with which their observations could be recorded. Each of these requirements represented a specific subtask for the schedule. Each subtask required a location in which it could be done, competent people to do it, and things to do it with. Knowing when to do each of the tasks was equally important.

The graduate students who proposed to test a hypothesis relating social interaction and purchasing behavior had to construct an operations schedule that satisfied the conflicting demands on their available material and personal resources (see Figure 2). The operations schedule shown in Figure 2 specifies four preliminary tasks. The fifth task, that of observing and tallying behaviors, becomes possible only as the result of the previous activities. Without a systematic way of describing and documenting the preliminary steps, the research procedures are

9

Figure 2. Operations Schedule for University District Craft Fair Study—October 9-10

Task	Subtask	Location	Staff	Materials	Time
1. Obtain observation site	a. Define criteria for selection	Class	Team		September 15
	b. Select site according to criteria	Tour fair area, site visits	Team	Written list of criteria	September 21
	c. Obtain permission to use site		Lori and Bob	Introductory letter from Dr. Wills, description of research activities	September 30
	(1) Contact bookstore manager	Bookstore office, other site offices			
	(2) Contact alternative sites				
2. Obtain data collection forms	a. Design tally form	Class	Team	Design specification	September 18
	b. Human Subjects Committee approval	Dean's office	Alice and Dr. Wills	Draft, design statement	September 21 (allow ten days for committee action)
	c. Produce forms	Mimeo room	Sam	Draft, approval certificate, budget number	October 2 at least—allow five to seven days
3. Schedule work periods	a. Make up schedule	Class	Tully		October 6
	b. List observers and alternates	Class	Tully		
	c. Notify team members of assignments	Class or homes	Tully, Julie	Phone numbers	October 7 (reminder calls evenings October 8 and 9)
4. Set up site	a. Align booths	Fair streets	Team	Site plan	12:00 midnight to 7:00 a.m., October 9 and 10; must be ready by 8:00 a.m.
	b. Arrange observation area	Bookstore office	Team	Tally sheets, pencils, binoculars, clipboards, chairs	9:00 a.m., October 9 and 10
	c. Clean office windows	Bookstore office	Team	Cleaning solution, water rags	9:00 a.m., October 9

much more difficult and are subject to confusion and contamination. The operations schedule provides a map for traversing the ill-defined paths of field research. Underlying the schedule is the concept of time.

Concepts of Time

Two kinds of time consideration enter into planning: questions of occurrence and of duration. Occurrence refers to chronological time, hours and dates. Time schedules must take account of holidays and special events—not only legal holidays but the local or regional celebrations that affect the usual activities of subjects and organizations. Accommodating to such events may be quite straightforward, such as remembering not to call people to a meeting on the Fourth of July, or not to ask teachers to participate in a workshop during school hours. Other dates may be excluded for less obvious reasons, related to special characteristics of the individual or situation; for example, mealtimes in the community must be respected.

Knowing something about the religious or cultural calendar of the area in which you will work is also necessary. Scheduling activities on Good Friday or Jewish High Holy Days may deprive you of the contributions of valuable subjects or staff members. Planning to conduct a street-corner traffic count during Asian Awareness Week might seriously skew the data (with the direction of the skew depending on where the count is taken). In addition to checking a conventional calendar and a calendar of special or cultural events, skim the neighborhood newspapers, which feature garage sales, church celebrations, and local school programs or athletic events. During a preliminary visit to the site, inspect bulletin boards and store windows that display advertisements and posters of coming events. Lists of events and dates can usually also be found in such publications as the brochures of the local chamber of commerce and tourist information office, as well as in the entertainment guides supplied by hotels and restaurants in most larger communities. If

11

there is a fairground, stadium, or exhibition hall in the community, check its schedule of attractions as well. A circus or a once-yearly major sports event can draw enormous crowds and interfere with the plans and with the people you expect to carry them out. The local police can usually provide estimates of crowd size and traffic conditions.

Fieldwork often requires activities outside the usual 8-to-5 working hours of most institutions. Not only must you find staff members who will work at these odd hours but you must also make special preparations for what will be done. Access to buildings and the ordinary support services that your parent organization provides (such as telephones and people to answer them) are unlikely to be available after hours or on weekends. In such situations, you may need to carry a supply of change at all times for telephone calls, station someone at a locked door to admit subjects who may arrive earlier or later than planned, and arrange to have equipment or materials hand-delivered from one experimenter to another when no central location for storing them is open. In areas where there are questions of safety, you might organize escort services after certain hours or select staff members who have the physical ability to protect themselves and their subjects.

Questions of duration pose different problems. At the most basic level, you must allow adequate time to conduct the research activities. Time must be calculated to include both the actual time occupied by the research task and the staging or preparatory time needed to set up and secure the work. For example, assume that subjects will be asked to evaluate the desirability of a number of sales presentations under actual floor conditions in a large department store. The observations themselves may take only a few minutes and scoring the rating sheets less than a minute longer. This five-minute period, however, is only a part of the fieldwork. The observers must be brought to the store, given their score sheets, and assigned to a particular department and salesperson before their research task starts; and they must be escorted from the site, relieved of their data collection forms, and sent on their way afterward—all before the researcher is free to introduce another group of observers to the experiment. The time for such a project may have to be counted in this way:

Experimenter 1   3:30   Transport first group of observers to store.

Experimenter 2   4:00   Meet subjects at door. Take them to fourth-floor shoe department.

Experimenter 1   4:00   Begin collection of second group of observers.

Experimenter 2   4:05   Place first group of observers at assigned points. Review instructions.

                  4:10-4:15   Observation.

                  4:15-4:18   Record scores.

                  4:19   Collect rating sheets.

                  4:20   Escort observers to door.

                  4:25   Meet second observer group.

Experimenter 1   4:25-4:55   Return first observers to their homes.

If Experimenter 1 and 2 are the same person, additional time for parking, travel, and breaks should be allowed. The five-minute task, under these quite typical field conditions, can take well over an hour of the researcher's time. If this expanded allowance of time runs over meal hours, or normal workdays, the project must provide for the comfort and convenience of the staff and participants. In such instances, the costs of food and hotel rooms must be balanced against the difficulty and the lost time involved in assembling the group more than once.

The operations schedule, then, allows you to specify what must be done and the conditions under which the activities can be carried out. It is not inflexible. Each of the tasks will affect subsequent ones, and conditions will change as the work progresses and you learn more about the actual field situation. Do not make changes, however, without carefully projecting the effect they will have on other parts of the work. Each change should be entered in the appropriate place in the schedule and the alterations carried forward. Thus, if you find that you must move a particular activity from one location to another, remember that this move may require more than changing a building's name on the instruction sheets. It will affect the distances people must travel and the time it takes to make the trip. It may mandate a different kind of transport, which in turn may change the qualifications of the staff members responsible for that part of the work. Say, for example, that you planned a workshop for twelve factory foremen, who afterward were to join other participants for a company-wide demonstration program at an industrial park. The original schedule called for the workshop to be held at the park's display building, but the building was not yet cleared of an import-export fair that had been held the previous day. Even assuming that you found alternative space for the workshop in another building several miles away, you had not yet solved all the problems that the change in plan created. Since the workshop participants could not simply walk across the park to the demonstration site, you had to find transportation for them. If they were driving their own cars, some of them could have straggled in late, and you would have needed parking both at the new location and at the demonstration. If it were possible to transport the group together in a van or bus, you would have had to arrange to rent or borrow this vehicle, remembering to obtain the proper insurance. How long would such a trip take? You had to make allowance for this extra time, either by starting your workshop earlier or by cutting out a portion of the program. Who could drive the van or bus? Did the staff member assigned to this duty have the required license, or did a driver have to be hired? Where could the vehicle be parked during the meeting? If parking space was available, was a special permit sticker needed? If it was a metered space, did the driver have change for the meter?

14

Planning for Field Operations

The answers to these questions became entries in the schedule, and these entries determined still other activities. It is the operations schedule that maintains order in such situations.

The schedule you establish for a project, however, must also account for times when research is not being done. You cannot expect your study to run smoothly and continuously from beginning to end. There will be periods when nothing is being done because no activities are scheduled for those times; at other times, the planned activities may be halted by errors or failure. To deal with such periods, you should introduce into the schedule two elements: estimated down time and built-in delay days. Down time is the period when work is halted by design. It may be the months between waves of a longitudinal study, the days you must wait between administering a test and receiving its results, or the weeks that elapse before you receive some piece of equipment that has been ordered. The operations schedule should include these periods, with special care that it does not move on to another part of the work without allowing adequate time for the previous steps to be completed. During down time, you may be able to leave the site of the research, perhaps to work on some other project. Remember, however, that down time is subject to inertia. You cannot expect to start again at full speed, as if there had never been a pause. Allow enough time to work up to running rate.

Down time is planned delay. Sometimes, however, the project will slow down or halt because something has gone wrong. To deal with these problems, you should add some un-specified delay time to the overall estimates; that is, in planning the exact length of time for each portion of the study, add some fixed percentage for loss. This extra allowance of time is entered on the operations schedule as part of the original esti-mate; for example, a conference presentation estimated to take four days to prepare (say, June 12 through June 15) appears on the schedule as occupying five days (June 12 through June 16). The extra time is added at the end of the time period, so that, if it is not needed, it can be carried forward to the next element or used to start some later procedure ahead of schedule. The flexibility it affords is very important. If the allowance is not used, you can rejoice in the luxury of having more time than you need. This is a rare occurrence and should be savored.

How these flexible time allowances can be used is shown in the following example. A social worker was assigned the task of evaluating the effectiveness of women's assertiveness classes offered by a number of educational and service groups. The classes generally met once each week for eight to twelve weeks. She decided that she would attend the first and last class of each series, administering a test of social competence each time and using the differences in self-perceived competence before and after the training as the measure of effectiveness. To test for persistence, she would administer the same competence test in a telephone interview eight to ten weeks after the final session. At this time, the subjects would also be asked to report in their own words what changes they had made in their actions and what effects they attributed to the new behavior. Eight classes, each registering at least ten but no more than sixteen partici-pants, were selected for evaluation. The researcher prepared the following time schedule:

March 1-March 31	Contact agencies, set up class schedule, correspond with subjects, obtain permission for study.
April 1-April 15	Pretest administration in first classes.
May 27-July 8	Posttest administration in last classes.
July 15-August 26	Telephone interviews.
September 21	Presentation of report.

Preparation for the study—that is, setting up meetings with the instructors and sponsors of the classes, obtaining permission from the women registered, constructing the interview schedule, and making arrangements to travel to the classes—was expected to take no less than four weeks. The researcher realized that these tasks might actually take longer but knew they had to be completed before the first class meeting on April 1. The researcher actually planned to have all the organizational and preparatory work done by March 28, but she added three delay days to the schedule. In fact, the preliminary tasks extended several days longer than the researcher had expected. Her delay days, however, provided the necessary extension of time, and she was ready when the classes met.

The two weeks between April 1 and 15 were assigned to data collection. The time after April 15 and before the posttest was designated as down time. In fact, the start of several of the classes was postponed, so that collection of the original data extended into the latter part of April. The social worker had planned other activities for that interval but· was forced to curtail them. Although she maintained her schedule on the research project, her other work fell behind. This situation was exacerbated during the second data collection period, since the classes that had started late also finished late. The anticipated down time between July 8 and 15 was taken up in completing the posttest. Because this week was available, however, the data collection could be kept on schedule. Six weeks had been allotted to the interviewing, estimated at the rate of about twenty half-hour interviews each week. Since the researcher actually planned to work faster than this, she was able to build in up to ten delay days, which she expected to use for a vacation. Her estimates of the pace of interviewing were accurate; what she had not anticipated was the late start of several groups. Since her design specified a twenty-week interval between first class and telephone interview, she was forced to wait until the end of August to contact some subjects, a time which conflicted with their vacations and hers. Her report was ready on September 21, but only barely. The week to ten days of delay time, which she had hoped would allow her to revise and polish the report, were lost, but including them in her plans at the beginning gave her the time she needed to complete her task. The operations schedule she had prepared became the structure on which the changes in her plans could be arranged.

Field Research

The examples in this chapter illustrate the essential organizing characteristic of the operations plan. The plan is a framework on which research is constructed, not a rigid cage in which it must be confined. It is important to have a clear conception of the underlying structure of the work but equally important to know how changes can be fitted in—and what effects the alterations will have on each succeeding activity. Showing both the original plans and their modifications in an organized array permits you to keep track of where your project started and where it is going. Without this information, managing field research is almost impossible.

Two

Research Sites and Settings

◆◆◆

Research must be done somewhere. The type of location depends on the design of the study. Among the places that meet your research specifications, you will need to find out which are available, convenient, and most efficient in furthering the work. Included in these considerations should be questions of ease of access, proximity to transportation and other services, safety, shelter, and comfort. You must be able to use space when you need it; bring in the necessary people and materials; store supplies until they are wanted; and provide the researchers, their subjects, and their equipment with protection against weather, physical discomfort, and danger.

Authorization for the use of space is still another matter. Places may be public, institutionally owned or managed, or private. In each of these cases, the right to use the place rests with some individual or organization from whom permission, implicit or explicit, must be obtained. Even street corners, parks, and other public places are under the management of officials, who must be at least notified of the research activities if the work is to go 'smoothly. You may be sure of your right to accost passersby in the interest of science, but informing the local police, forest rangers, or security staff will certify your actions. It will also prevent embarrassing questions and interruptions from the attendant who wants to know why your field workers are recording the license numbers of cars at the Park and Ride Lot, the police officer who asks you to identify yourself as you are conducting a sidewalk interview, and the school officials who are justifiably suspicious of strangers speaking to children at the schoolyard gate. (See Chapter Three.)

When the research sites are actually owned by institutions or individuals, there are other procedures that must be followed. The owner or manager must give permission and must inform his or her representatives that you and your agents have this clearance. If the owner is not the occupant of the site, or if he or she is only one of many occupants, then permission must also be obtained from each occupant. Thus, it is not sufficient to obtain the cooperation of the owner or manager of a factory or institution before research can be conducted on the premises. The workers or residents who customarily use the spaces must also be informed. Utilization of the hospital's cafeteria requires not only that the manager agree but that the employees who are accustomed to eating there accept the diversion of "their" space to your purposes. In the usual course of field research, moreover, it is the occupants who are the study's subjects. You cannot afford to contaminate the research by hostility or uneasiness because the project, however worthy, has intruded on the subjects' usual patterns of going about their businesses.

Field research projects, of course, are usually planned in cooperation with the organization on whose premises the work will take place. Under these circumstances, there is no difficulty in obtaining authorization from the management. Other groups or individuals, however, must still be approached. For example, the personnel division of Apex Corporation received authorization from the board of directors and the general manager to cooperate with a faculty member in industrial design at Central University, and with a graduate student whom he was sponsoring, to conduct a study of the effective utilization of in-plant resource maintenance record forms. The design of the study postulated that improved flow management of materials would result in noticeable production economies. The operations schedule listed the following tasks: training employees in the use of the forms, monitoring their distribution, collecting and recording data, and measuring the efficiency of purchasing and storage procedures affected by the new system. The necessary locations, then, would be within the plant and would include meeting rooms, observation points in the work areas, and desk and record storage space associated with the purchasing office of the company.

In this instance, allocation of all the needed spaces was within the manager's authority. He agreed that the researchers could use the company cafeteria for training; a corner of the purchasing office for desk space; and the work floors for observation purposes. The researchers soon discovered, however, that the real control over these places was more complex than originally appeared. First of all, the assignment of space in the purchasing office required the office manager to have the needed desks and shelves cleared or brought in; he also had to provide the researchers with access to the area and its amenities. As a result, other employees had to be moved, the normal flow of work and conversation patterns reorganized, and some people deprived of the use of areas that they had claimed as their own. The effort involved was greater than that which would result from the simple addition of new employees. The researchers were different people, doing different work, which cut across, even if it did not actually impede, usual activities. Using the cafeteria was even more complicated. Although the

21

employees realized that they did not own it, they had come to regard it as their personal place during meals and coffee breaks. Most of them had staked claims to a particular corner or table, which they shared with their friends. Diverting the place to different uses might be seen as trespass. In the study described here, however, the company had made a practice of making the cafeteria available for community and service organizations' use. The employees, familiar with United Way breakfasts and Little League suppers in the facility, could accept other uses of the cafeteria without difficulty.

The most sensitive spaces were those on the work floor. An unspoken tradition had given the operator of a machine authority over the few square feet surrounding his or her work station. Even the foreman hesitated a short distance away until the worker's recognition gave him implicit permission to approach. While this tradition had certain safety benefits in preventing the operator from sudden distraction or loss of concentration during sometimes dangerous procedures, it was actually seen as an acknowledgment of the worker's authority over his station. The walkways between stations, however, were common to all employees. As an added difficulty, the contract between the company and the workers' union stipulated in great detail the allowable supervision procedures. A researcher moving about the plant and recording the times and ways in which employees used the forms under study might easily be seen as threatening to the workers and their union.

The resolution of these questions required the cooperation of management, the union, employees, and the research team. The researchers had to obtain the support of the workers, but they were concerned that too much publicity and information about the study would lead the subjects to act "for" the researchers, modifying their usual behavior to do what they thought was expected of them. (This is a familiar research problem. Ways of obtaining cooperation which do not tend to affect the validity of results are discussed in Chapter Three.)

During the planning for the study, the researchers decided to add another element. Because the acceptability of the forms was also under study, and because the employees might give more open evaluations if they were asked to respond off company premises, the researchers decided to interview employees at the employees' homes. This requirement, that the research activity take place in privately owned or used places, introduced a third type of location. Private places are under the control of individuals. (Some methods for gaining the permission of owners or residents also are presented in Chapter Three.)

In the course of preparing for their study, these researchers had to find suitable facilities for all their planned activities. Therefore, on their operations schedule (see Figure 3), they

Figure 3. Operations Schedule for Resource Management Study

Task	Subtask	Location
1. Train employees	a. Prepare training instructions	U. Press will edit—bring copy to Rm. 112 in Communications Building
	b. Select training site	Company cafeteria
2. Monitor distribution		Tool cribs (foreman will introduce us to keeper)
3. Monitor recording	a. Select observation points	Tour plant to identify points (clear with union representatives)
	b. Monitor use of forms	Selected machine stations
4. Monitor collection	a. Observe turn-in	Tool cribs
	b. Tally and record	Tool cribs and office
5. Collect data on efficiency	a. Select data points	Manager's office and staff conference room
	b. Collect data from records	Purchasing Office desk
6. Survey of workers' opinions	a. Obtain home addresses	Personnel Office (request interview appointment)
	b. Request interviews	Telephone from U. office
	c. Conduct interviews	Employees' homes

23

noted the required type of location beside each activity, the name or title of the person authorized to give permission for its use, and the procedure that must be followed, such as "Obtain letter of approval from manager" or "Request interview appointment." They also left space for further details, since they would have to enter information on any changes or special procedures needed to make the chosen space usable.

Adapting and Utilizing the Site

For each activity on the operations schedule, the proper setting must be assured. Few field settings are intrinsically suitable for research activities, and ordinarily you will not be permitted to make permanent or substantial physical changes. By temporary manipulations of space and equipment, however, you can create the environment that the work requires.

The problems to be solved are practical ones, revolving around such questions as "Who has the key to the building after 5:00 p.m.?" "Where can the members of the research team go to eat lunch?" "Where can we lock up the meters between test periods?" "If we choose this west window because it is best placed for observation, how can we avoid being blinded by the afternoon sun?" or "How can we make sure that only one subject at a time sees the display?" These are not trivial issues. The research design must be filtered through people, equipment, and settings not necessarily best suited to the work. The less you are distracted by inconveniences, the more you will be able to concentrate your efforts on the study itself. An example:

The board of directors of an inner-city community center —in order to support an application for new staff positions and renovation of the building—wanted documentation for their contention that the facilities were being used in excess of their capacity. The city's Department of Youth Services claimed, however, that the center had failed to enforce regulations requiring users either to possess valid membership cards or to purchase day-use tickets. Instead, the critics charged, the center

24

allowed people to lend their cards to others, admitted more than one person on a single ticket, and let people who had come in as spectators use the facilities and equipment. The center's staff explained that their policies were deliberately lax because they wanted to get as many young people as possible involved in the center's activities. The staff realized that more precise data on the actual level of use were necessary but were unwilling to divert money from operations for this purpose. In this impasse, a member of the board, who taught sports and recreation at the community college, offered to recruit students to take a count of visitors and participants at the center. Her offer was accepted, and she agreed to have the students there on three evenings and two weekend days during the next month. The center manager planned the study to include a check of membership cards at the entrance; a brief interview with entrants, to determine which facility they planned to use; and a longer interview with every fifteenth person to pass the turnstiles. Ticket purchasers would be interviewed at the cashier's window. Participants, visitors, and spectators entered the building through four adjoining doors. The cashier's cage was set outside the doors. The doorways opened into a lobby, from which the entrants were channeled through turnstiles—three for use by members and the fourth for collection of day-use tickets and spectator passes. During the study, two of the turnstiles were locked, leaving only one each for members and others. The director set up narrow tables across the lobby, and entrants had to file past the tables to reach the turnstile. A student was stationed at each table to ask which facility would be used. While the entrant was answering, another student at the members' turnstile checked the membership card against a printout roster of all members. Those whose names were not listed were asked to go back to the cashier to buy a ticket or to go to the office to request an exemption from the director. At the other turnstile, one student asked about the use of facilities, and another tallied the tickets or passes turned in. Beyond the turnstiles, interviewers waited to stop every fifteenth person. Another

25

interviewer stood at the cashier's cage outside the door. Under these makeshift conditions, the researchers attempted to conduct their study on the first evening. For the early arrivals, the procedures worked smoothly. As the numbers entering the building increased, however, delays began to build up. Entrants, meeting their friends in the lobby and eager to begin activities, milled around, pushing against the tables, refusing to answer questions, and shoving their way to the turnstiles. There, many became angry at the unusually strict control of tickets and cards. In the poor light, searching for names on the printout went very slowly. Youths who had been accustomed to getting in free simply jumped over the locked turnstiles or pushed their way through. The student interviewers were ignored, except by one burly young man, who—infuriated when his outdated card was confiscated—leaped over the barrier, grabbed a handful of questionnaires, and tore them up. Meanwhile, the interviewer outside, watching her questionnaires smear in the rain, gave up her efforts and came inside for shelter. By 8 p.m. the crush in the lobby had dissipated; and the director, the faculty member, and her students could assess the problems. Two major sources of difficulty were identified. The first, and less serious, related to the physical arrangements of the area. The next evening that the study was conducted, sturdy crowd-control fences were set up across the lobby, the additional turnstiles were opened, and stronger light bulbs were placed in the ceiling fixtures. The barriers were extended to the doorway, so that people entered the building in lines rather than as a mob. Counselors stood at the doorways, allowing people to enter no faster than they cleared the turnstiles at the other end of the lobby. Free of the crowding, the entrants were more willing to speak to the interviewers. A sheltered spot was found for the interviewer outside. Signs were posted at the door and in the lobby, explaining the study and asking for cooperation.

The more serious problem had to do with the basic approach to the research. At the outset, the board members, the director, and to some extent even the faculty member did not acknowledge that resources would be necessary. Inadequate preparations were made, and the study was starved of both planning and effort. By attempting to do the work with the least amount of bother to themselves, the researchers made it almost impossible to do at all.

Managing people is more complex than simply making sure they enter the right door and are not allowed to move the furniture out of position. Research design often demands that access to and contact with and between subjects take place only under stringent controls. It may be necessary to shield an individual entering the research condition from one who has already undergone the experience, to keep some subjects from observing what occurs during certain stages, and to prevent subjects from learning about the experimental procedures before their turn to participate. Under laboratory conditions, such controls are facilitated by the laboratory setting itself. Multiple entrances, soundproofing, separated waiting rooms and cubicles, one-way glass, and other physical controls can be provided. In the field, the settings are less amenable to your needs.

The controls that the study requires must often be improvised. The setting, the research staff members, and the materials can all be utilized to create the necessary conditions of control. It may be possible to locate spaces or rooms where the access can be managed with minimal trouble. Locking one or more of a number of doors, for example, or closing curtains can effectively isolate a particular area. Partitions, screens, or even a row of desks can be situated to direct and concentrate people in the right places. Such space dividers need not even be physical. A line of tape laid down the center of a corridor, arrows chalked or painted on a wall, or directional signs may be adequate to show people the paths they should follow. These optical cues, however, will not prevent people from mingling in open areas and sharing their experiences. More direct means are required to separate groups.

A rope stretched between posts or a line of folding chairs marks a boundary but still permits the exchange of information

27

across it. Moreover, subjects entering the research area will be curious and perhaps apprehensive. They will peer through a momentarily opened door, strain to hear sounds or voices from nearby rooms, and anxiously ask each other what is about to happen. Well-known studies have made use of these factors in several ways. For instance, the investigators have "planted" confederates to give subjects supposedly casual information, which is in reality part of the experimental manipulation; or they have exposed the subjects to sights or sounds which, without their knowledge, are part of the experiment. Where this is part of your design, the shortcomings of the setting may be deliberate. Be sure, however, that you do not inadvertently build these elements into the study by failing to control the spaces and the people who use them.

Selecting an Independent Site

When field research is done in cooperation with organizations or institutions, the site of the study is usually supplied. The industrial study described took place primarily inside the subject plant. The employee interviews which were part of the project were held at the respondents' homes. The rationale for the use of both of these locations was inherent in the design. Frequently, however, a space is needed which is controlled by individuals or institutions not related to the research itself. Under these circumstances, the researchers must find an appropriate place on their own and arrange for its use.

A wide variety of facilities are available in most communities. Hotels have meeting rooms to rent; colleges and other schools may lend the use of classrooms, theaters, or conference rooms; many church schoolrooms stand empty during the week; and banks, libraries, utility companies, and similar public and semipublic organizations frequently have rooms that can be used. There may be no charge, or a token fee to cover maintenance may be collected, or the researcher might be asked to pay a substantial amount. The chamber of commerce or public library in most communities has information about available space. It is tempting to select the cheapest accommodation. There are times, however, when an expensive site is well worth the cost—for instance, when it serves to identify the research with a prestigious organization or, at least, avoids identifying it with questionable ones. Another factor to be considered is the comfort and safety of the participants. An example:

A faculty member in the college of engineering at an urban university received a research grant to investigate public attitudes toward the safety criteria required in selecting the sites for nuclear power plants. Much of the data would be collected through opinion surveys. During the planning for the survey in an outlying area, the researcher had to select the place where interviewers could be trained. They would come to a central location from a radius of fifty to a hundred miles on a Saturday morning. Conversations with local businessmen and community officials gave leads to a number of rooms that might be available. The researcher called or visited the persons in charge of these places, obtained information on the facilities they offered, and, in some cases, inspected the rooms. Based on considerations of size, facilities, and location, she identified five possible sites.

1. A conference room in the school district's administration building could be made available. Using it would require paying the wages of a custodian to open and close the building. At a required minimum of four hours, overtime, the cost would be approximately $50. Ample parking was nearby.

2. A telephone call to the chamber of commerce produced information that a popular local steak house had a room used for service club luncheons during the week and for parties at other times. As a public convenience, the owner offered this room free for community meetings.

3. The water company had an auditorium at its headquarters. This was located several miles from the center of town, on a wooded tract in the watershed area. The room had frequently been used for community meetings at no charge.

The setting of the building was beautiful, in well-maintained parkland.

4. The Evangelical Church volunteered free use of a discussion room in its Sunday school building. A room of adequate size, furnished with easy chairs and small tables as a coffee lounge, was next to the nursery school quarters, in use on the meeting day.

5. The community college library's film-viewing room was available. There was no rental fee, but the researcher would be asked to pay a token fee of $10 for maintenance. The college cafeteria and parking lot would be open.

In choosing among these possible locations, the researcher had to consider the convenience of the facilities themselves and the possible effect of the location on her work. She felt that the restaurant room, while centrally located and free, would lack the atmosphere of scientific investigation she wanted associated with her project. Similarly, the church lounge seemed not sufficiently businesslike. The arrangement of the room, with comfortable chairs set around a fireplace, did not appear conducive to the formal training program she planned. In addition, since the interviewer candidates were all housewives, and most were mothers, she feared that the presence of the children's activities next door might distract the proceedings.

Of all the possibilities, the water company's auditorium seemed at first the most eligible. The company's community service division offered assistance in setting up the meeting; and the room's facilities, as described in a brochure supplied by the public relations office, were excellent. One thing, however, caught the researcher's attention as she read the brochure. A list of the public uses to which the auditorium had been put included no activities within the previous two years, although the brochure had been recently reprinted. The researcher mentioned this to several people in the town and was told that the park was now heavily used by motorcycle racers on weekends and that some vandalism of cars in the parking lots had been reported.

Research Sites and Settings

The remaining two sites were both associated with educational institutions, were centrally located, and offered adequate facilities. The choice, then, could be made simply on economic grounds. The meeting was successfully held at the community college.

After you have tentatively chosen a suitable place, you must inspect it more closely, to determine whether in fact it lends itself to your use. Potential problems can usually be avoided by a simple process, which should become an absolute rule: Before committing the project to the site, "walk through" the procedures; that is, review each activity in terms of the actual steps that must be taken. The first walk-through should be a mental one. Outline the procedures, in scenario form, and read through them carefully, to note any inconsistencies or awkwardness. Is a single researcher scheduled to perform two tasks simultaneously? Have you allowed for late arrivals to the experimental site? Does the location in fact lend itself to the experimental manipulation you have planned? Where discrepancies appear, reconcile them in the statement of design and methodology.

After you have satisfied yourself that the procedures and requirements are possible, according to the written plans, translate the review to the site, paying attention to traffic patterns, doorways, light and ventilation, furniture and equipment. Stop at each step to observe what you are doing. Raise such questions as these: "I hand out the questionnaires here. Is there a table on which to place them while I demonstrate how to fill them out?" "The group members form into committees at this point. Do they go to different parts of the room for their discussions, or do they simply turn away from each other?" "Are other rooms available?" "Are the chairs movable?" "If I time the discussions, how many minutes shall I allow for the observers to walk from one site to another, to signal starting and stopping times?" What problems might this inspection reveal? Some examples:

A group of subjects were to meet as a panel in a rural state. The most convenient geographical location was the auditorium of the local Grange hall, a large, bare room with windows along one wall and a small stage taking up most of one end. The furniture consisted of folding chairs, although two small tables were available as well. The main door opened onto an unpaved parking lot. Because most of the prospective panel members were employed, the meeting was held on a Saturday, when the offices of the Grange organization, in a separate wing of the building, were closed.

In their original review of the plans, the researchers noted several potential problems. The building was four miles from the nearest town, on a county road. None of the regular employees would be on hand to give information or assistance. While residents of the immediate area were familiar with the Grange hall, those arriving from other parts of the region would not know how to reach it. Arrangements to meet these difficulties could be made in advance. A map was prepared, showing the best route to the site from the major highways. A plan of the building itself showed the parking lot and the entrance to be used. Copies of the map and floor plan were sent to all the attendees, along with the meeting announcement. The researchers made sure that they could obtain the auditorium key during working hours on the preceding day; they also arranged for its return to the home of an employee in the evening. Because of the distance from town, the meeting announcement also contained the suggestion that attendees might wish to bring a sack lunch to eat at the building.

During the on-site walk-through, however, a number of other problems were noted. The water fountain serving the auditorium was out of order, and the coffee maker and vending machine used by the employees were not accessible from the meeting area. The stage area was discovered to be extremely deep, raising question about whether the speakers' voices would be heard without amplification. In addition, one of the researchers felt strongly that the relationship between the research team and the panel would be distorted if the researchers had to address panel members from a stage, rather than meeting with them on an equal level in discussion format. To meet this objection, the researchers decided to rearrange the folding chairs in the room, so that everyone could sit together. However, these chairs had no arms, so that writing during the session might be very difficult. The research team considered the alternative advantages of setting up tables or providing clipboards for the group. Eventually, the researchers decided to request additional tables and to arrange the chairs about them in a hollow square, with the meeting's speakers along one side. Instructional materials, supplies, and the slide projector would be placed on a table directly behind the speakers. One of the researchers agreed to bring in a supply of water, soft drinks, ice, and a coffee urn with cups, sugar, and cream for refreshment during meeting breaks and lunch.

Given this advance preparation, the research team did not expect to find serious problems interfering with their work. In fact, only three difficulties arose. Team members arrived early at the auditorium, unlocked the building with the key they obtained the previous day, and brought in their supplies and equipment. The tables they had requested were in the room, folded and stacked against the wall. The researchers began to set up the tables and arrange the chairs; they were assisted by a few of the subjects, who had also come early. As others drifted in, they also helped. The slight confusion and bustle these activities caused was unimportant and probably served to alleviate tension and increase the ease of the group. During this time, however, one of the researchers set the discussion materials on a table and then moved away to assist the others. A few of the newly arrived attendees very naturally wandered over to the table and began reading some of the materials, which they should not have seen until a late stage in the meeting. Fortunately, one of the researchers noticed this and quickly retrieved the material, covering the remainder to prevent similar incidents.

By the time scheduled for the start of the meeting, the room was in order, with subjects seated in their places, waiting for the last few attendees to arrive. It was at this moment that another problem arose. One of the subjects who had helped move the tables noticed that her hands were dirty and asked where the bathroom was, so that she could wash them. A local resident said that the toilets were in the basement of the building, down a stair which led from the main entry hall. The key to this part of the building had not been supplied. The researchers, however, had the name and address of an employee living nearby. While they began the meeting, one of the team went there for the proper key. The group accepted these incidents in good humor and shared in the momentary anxiety and relief of discovering first that the slide projector cord was not quite long enough to reach the wall socket and then that an extension cord had been packed in the supply box.

The single problem that caused the most serious disruption was a factor not of the research location itself but of the nearby community. The research team had visited the area on a weekday and did not realize that on Saturday the neighboring farm families made their weekly excursion to town. The three small restaurants were jammed between 11:00 and 1:30, and the attendees who chose to go into town for their lunch were delayed in returning. The afternoon session started over an hour late.

Establishing a Field Headquarters

In addition to the setting for actual research, it is often necessary to establish an office or a location from which the work can be managed. The study itself may take only a few days or hours, but weeks of preparation before and between the research periods may be required for setting up and maintaining the project. Deciding whether to manage a study from your home office, hire a local manager and obtain space at the research site, or pay the cost of maintaining one or more members of a research group at the site depends on questions of cost and opportunity. Over short distances, it might be most feasible for researchers to travel to the site whenever necessary, while keeping the management of the study at their home organization. Where greater distances are involved, or where a number of people will be recruited to work on the study, an office at the site might prove both economical and efficient. And under other circumstances, sending a group of researchers to live at the site until their work is done might be the best decision. Moreover, all of these methods might be used on a single project. An example:

A university-based survey research organization was commissioned to conduct a study of opinion on health care facilities in four areas of the state. These sites included the central area of the city where the university was located; a suburb of a neighboring city, about forty miles away; a rural farming area centering on a medium-sized marketing community in the center of the state; and a sparsely populated coastal strip, dependent on summer visitors for its income. In each of the four sites, a team of interviewers would have to be trained and supervised as they conducted interviews with sample households over a three-month period. In the university's home city this presented no problem. All of the facilities for recruiting, training and managing the work of the interviewers were available, with experienced staff members already in place. The other three locations, however, posed some problems.

For the nearby suburban district, part of the problem was easily solved. One of the organization's staff members usually commuted to work from the selected suburb, and she was delighted with the opportunity to set up a survey office in her spare bedroom and do most of her work at home. She was not experienced in the actual supervision of a field staff, but her knowledge about basic survey operations made it likely that she would rapidly become an efficient local supervisor. The university arranged to install an extra telephone in her home for conduct of the survey and to hire a cleaning service to maintain the room, which would be used as a semipublic office. A share of the total heat and lighting bills was to be prorated and charged

Field Research

to the project. Since much of the fieldwork on a survey takes place during evenings and on weekends, the woman found it very convenient to be at home when her interviewers would be most likely to need her help. Daily telephone contact and regular trips into the home office helped her to maintain a high quality of work in her district. Her occasional requests for assistance could be easily met by sending out an experienced staff member from the organization for a few hours to work with her.

In the other two locations, however, the survey organization was not so fortunate. The small city in the farming area had no research facility, and no resident seemed willing or able to direct the work locally. After a careful consideration of comparative costs, the researchers decided to establish an office and move a staff member to the city, rather than attempting to direct work there from 150 miles away. One of the research assistants agreed to move to the smaller city for the duration of the study. An early visit to the city showed that little housing or office space was available and that there was no local transportation. The research assistant found a vacant store on the main street, however, that would be suitable as an office; and a small apartment, barely furnished, was located a few blocks away. Both were available on a monthly lease. The assistant's personal belongings and essential furniture were moved on the university's truck, which also brought basic office furniture, equipment, and supplies to the new location. Within a few days, the research office was set up and ready for interviewing and selecting the applicants who responded to advertisements in the local newspaper and other recruiting appeals. In this case, the experienced assistant needed little help from the organization in training and supervising her interviewers. An occasional telephone call clarified any problems, and her weekly call to report progress rarely required any action. The interviewers picked up assignments and brought completed work to the storefront office at regular office hours. During the course of the study, the assistant made friends with several of them and frequently visited their homes or went to social affairs with them and their families. (It should be noted that the assistant's primary purpose in volunteering to manage the study was not achieved. She had visualized it as a quiet, isolated time during which she could complete her dissertation. The work of setting up the survey, followed by the active social life she was urged to join, left her little time to write.) At the end of the study period, she dismantled her office, and the furniture and equipment were sent back to the university, along with the final data from the project.

For the scattered residents of the seacoast area, however, there was no population center from which the survey could be mounted. The study took place in the autumn and winter, and most of the motels and summer cabins along the beaches were empty. A group of graduate students from the university, trained as interviewers, conducted the fieldwork on the survey, staying a few weeks at a time in each of several vacation colonies. The permanent residents of the area, with little work to do during the off-season, were accessible and cooperative, and the study was completed in good time.

Each of these solutions was a response to a particular set of local requirements and resources. A field study may need nothing more than a busy street corner, but much more complex arrangements usually must be made. Decisions on the kind of location are based on the design of the research. Selecting which of the places that meet the specifications depends on considerations of convenience and economy.

Three

Communications, Information, and Authorization

◆▸◆▸ ◆▸◆▸ ◆▸ ◆▸◆▸ ◆▸ ◆▸◆▸ ◆▸ ◆▸◆▸ ◆▸ ◆▸◆▸ ◆▸◆

Individuals and organizations participate in research for a number of reasons. The subjects may have a real interest in furthering scientific investigation, but it is common for them to participate primarily because they believe the research will benefit either themselves or causes that they support. It is even more common for them to agree out of simple courtesy and desire to help the researcher who asks their assistance. Nevertheless, people seek to protect themselves against inconvenience and discomfort, and institutions take very seriously their responsibility to guard their clients. Convincing them to cooperate, either personally or by permitting the research to be conducted in spaces they control, requires that you demonstrate the real or anticipated rewards that the work will produce.

Full acceptance into the community and the cooperation you receive will be based largely on what the community members know about you and your work. The information that is provided must be designed to serve the purposes of the study. No matter how prestigious your sponsor, your relations with community members—whether they are staff, subjects, or bystanders—are your responsibility. Your introduction to the community, the publicity that your study generates, and the reports on what is being done may emanate from your parent organization, but you will be accountable for what the community knows about the research. Winning acceptance and maintaining good local relations are important parts of your work. The problems of gaining credence are particularly acute for researchers working alone, although they exist to some extent in all fieldwork situations.

Authorization

Researchers carry differing degrees of credibility into the community. Whether you and your project are accepted depends both on the value of the work itself and on your ability to present it to its designated audience. You will need acceptance and authorization from two groups: (1) the subjects whom you want to participate and (2) the owners or managers on whose premises, or through whose support, you want your project to be conducted. Gaining their approval requires that they accept you and the institution or organization you represent. It is easiest to enter the community under the auspices of some known and respected institution. Students doing fieldwork will find it useful to operate under the sponsorship, or at least under the name, of their parent university, while researchers conducting field studies for governmental agencies may find it helpful to refer to the governmental unit in their public statements and written materials. Sometimes, of course, the name of the sponsoring agency can do more harm than good. Researchers investigating satisfaction with neighborhood home ownership during a campaign to change the property tax base, for instance, should be cautious in how they identify themselves. Even though their work is being done as part of a study of community development, the property owners may still suspect that their cooperation will result in higher taxes. In such circumstances, it is important to make clear the distinction between the office of community planning and the county tax assessor's division, or to stress some cosponsoring group, such as HUD or a state land-use agency. The sponsor should be identified by name, unless this information is likely to bias the results; in that case, it may be necessary to use terms that do not carry strong connotative associations. Thus, an investigation of racial bias during a school integration controversy should be associated with "several citizen public-interest groups" rather than the NAACP and ACLU. If asked, you must of course answer honestly, although it is possible to say, "I am not supposed to give out that information, because we don't want the study to be affected by what people may have heard about it already."

You can expect to be asked about the sponsorship of your study, and you may find it necessary to defend your association with the organization or to explain why you, as an individual unsupported by any socially recognized institution, should be given credence. Your relationship with your sponsor may be a delicate one. To some extent, the organization is responsible for your activities; but you, in turn, are also considered responsible for the organization. You will be the recipient of complaints and criticisms about the sponsor. If you represent a state agency, for instance, you may be asked what the legislature has done about insurance rates; if you represent a university, you may be asked why the subject's nephew wasn't admitted. Most of these comments can only be handled with patience and courtesy. Sometimes, however, you can provide

41

assistance or obtain answers to questions asked in the field. You should remember that, tenuous though your connection to the institution may be, it is still more direct than that of others.

Your relationship to your sponsor should be made apparent. Use of the organization's letterhead for your correspondence, seals or symbols on equipment and materials, and personal identification such as cards or badges can be very impressive. For short-term use, you may find it unnecessary to invest in elaborate materials. You can probably obtain gummed stickers with the appropriate name and logo to attach to notebooks or briefcases. An identification badge can be made with the staff member's name written on a card to which a seal has been pasted or on which the logo from a sheet of letterhead paper has been mounted. Such tokens carry a disproportionate weight in the field. They reassure both subjects 'and staff members. Since identifying yourself with an organization implies that the relationship will be acknowledged, you should arrange for your sponsorship to be verified. Your communications to the public should contain an address or telephone number at the institution where inquiries can be made, and you must be sure that whoever responds to these inquiries knows who you are and what you are doing in the field. It is very embarrassing to refer a subject to your parent organization for confirmation, only to discover that the secretary who answers the telephone has no idea of what your project is, while the office to which you report is closed for lunch. It is useful to provide a written description of your activities, to be used when inquiries are received. A note such as the following can be posted:

Memo to Departmental Secretaries
and Receptionists
Two of Professor Whealan's students are conducting a field count of meteorological installations in Southern Bell and Henderson Townships. The students are Tim Schallinger and Robert Grieves; they will be visiting farms and resorts between March 12

Communications, Information, and Authorization

and 26 to inspect rain and wind gauges maintained by the state weather service. The students carry university ID cards. Please inform any inquirers that the study is sponsored by the university. The department will send letters confirming the study to any residents who request them. *Be sure to get names and addresses if they do!* You may refer callers to Professor Whealan if they wish more information.

The field researcher working alone, of course, lacks such institutional support. He or she will have to obtain personal recommendations which are of equivalent respectability and make private arrangements for proving legitimacy. If you are conducting your fieldwork independently, gaining the authority which is provided by an institution may be impossible. Under these conditions, you must move very cautiously until your credentials are accepted. It will be especially important to obtain the support of some influential member of the community, who can smooth your entrance. You can expect to be repeatedly asked to demonstrate your competence and honorable intentions.

Authorization and Informed Consent

Only after you have satisfied the legitimate curiosity of the people you approach will you be authorized to begin your work. When these people give permission for themselves and for areas over which they have jurisdiction, the process is straightforward. Each individual is assumed to be qualified to choose what activities he or she will engage in. So-called "informed consent" is a special case of individual authorization. Informed consent stipulates that the subject has been made aware of precisely what will be involved in the research and has voluntarily agreed, after having the opportunity to consider the matter, to participate. To an increasing extent, research funded under gov-

43

ernmental and institutional support requires informed consent of all participants. You may be required to obtain a signed, notarized or witnessed letter of consent from the participants before any research activities can take place. The consent statement verifies that you have informed the subjects about what they will be asked to do and notified them of any risks involved in their tasks, and that they have accepted these. Even when written permission is impractical, the requirements are not relaxed. Verbal agreement for telephone or street corner interviews, for example, must be explicit. It is not enough to assume that the respondents will hang up or walk away if they do not wish to participate. In a discouragingly large proportion of cases, they do; but you must nevertheless verify the cooperation of those who do not. A formula that includes the essential elements of informed consent must precede every contact with a subject. There are at least five such elements: the subjects should be informed who you are, how they were selected for the study, that their inclusion is voluntary, what use will be made of the results, and what confidentiality provisions have been made for protecting the data. An introductory statement like this meets the stipulations:

> Good morning, I am a staff member of the Public Health Community Dentistry Program. We are interviewing people, picked at random at the clinic today, about their familiarity with dental care services in the city. The results of the survey will help the health department plan better dental care. Your participation is completely voluntary, and whether or not you are interviewed will not affect the health care you receive. Your responses will be held in confidence, and your name will not be used. The interview will take about five minutes. Do you have any questions I can answer?

If any aspects of the study do not conform to these conditions, they must be specifically indicated. Thus, the subjects

44

may have to be informed that you will record their name, but only for the purpose of mailing them a rating sheet later, or that verbatim excerpts from their statements may be anonymously reported. It may be awkward to ask subjects for permission in advance of their participation. For example, a respondent may be unwilling to sign a formal consent for an interview until after he has heard and considered his answers to the questions. In other instances, people observed in some natural setting are unlikely to continue behaving in an unstudied way after they have been informed that they are under observation. Under such circumstances, it may be necessary to first collect the data and then obtain authorization to use them. If permission is refused, the data will have to be discarded.

Your procedures for obtaining consent often must be specified in great detail before your study is approved. You may be instructed to follow the regulations set by the federal government or local research establishments. For the most part, these have been designed to protect subjects at risk in much more stringent experimental situations than your fieldwork is likely to present. Nevertheless, you may be bound by highly restrictive language. You must be prepared to demonstrate that your research offers no threat to its subjects and that the procedures you design are appropriate to the constraints of your work. It is much more difficult to apply formal consent procedures in the community than in the traditional laboratory setting. Handing out consent forms to be signed before the start of a laboratory experiment is a simple procedure. Driving forty miles over mountain roads to reach an isolated commune, for the purpose of requesting permission to return on another day to conduct an interview, is another matter. In fieldwork situations, you must design a system that will allow you to obtain consent at minimum cost to your project. Administering consent procedures is often viewed as an unreasonable constraint on research. In fact, the requirements of informed consent are no more than the precautions which a conscientious researcher will take in any case.

Field Research

The consent which you receive from individuals applies only to their own participation. In other instances, you will need to obtain consent from people who control access to the subjects. That is, you may need to contact parents; officials charged with management of organizations, such as school principals or hospital administrators; or those who have physical control over access, such as gatekeepers or building supervisors. You must apply to people in these positions for authorization to approach your intended subjects. It is common for people to assume control over access to which they are not actually entitled. The authorization you receive must be given by a person qualified to give it.

You may find that the right to permit activities resides in multiple layers of authority, only some of which have any official standing. Nevertheless, every one of the authorities must be approached and cleared. Bypassing a quasi-official authority is likely to result in passive resistance to your efforts. In extreme cases, violation of an implicit chain of command can deny access to subjects completely. For example:

An employee of the state historical society planned to conduct oral history interviews with the residents of a church-supported home for the aged. The board of directors of the home was enthusiastic about the project, and the pastor and church board also expressed interest and offered assistance in transcribing the interviews, to form part of the church archives. The researcher met with the director of the home, who gave permission and circulated a notice to her staff members, asking them to facilitate the study. The pastor mentioned the project in his weekly service in the home's chapel and described it again in the church newsletter. With authorization from the church and home, the historian felt that her project was well under way. She began her visits to the home with high expectations. Once there, however, she found it curiously hard to meet with the elderly residents. She was introduced to women just as they were summoned to their physical therapy sessions; she spent long periods waiting in the recreation room for gentlemen who, she later discovered, had dentist's appointments at the times she had arranged to talk to them; or she found herself seated at the bedside of a charming great-grandmother who spoke only Swedish. When she did talk to residents, they spoke little. After several weeks of such frustrations, she was invited to attend the annual luncheon of the ladies' guild. Over the meal, she mentioned the difficulties she was having. The women at the table, who had all worked as volunteers at the home, understood immediately. The home, they explained, was directed by a registered nurse and had other nurses and a social worker on the staff. The day-to-day care of the residents, however, was entrusted to practical nurses and aides, many of whom were poorly educated and concerned about their jobs. Any stranger entering the home and talking privately with residents was suspected of gathering complaints and reports of poor work. The researcher was seen as a threat to the staff members, and they attempted to limit her contacts with the residents. In addition to interfering with her schedule, they dropped casual remarks about how bored she would be by the grumbling and dull stories of the residents' youth and how difficult it would be to use the tape recorder. Overhearing these comments, many residents were too embarrassed to participate. The staff members had no official position in the hierarchy of the home, but their reluctance to accept the researcher made her work impossible.

The solution to the historian's problem was simple. At an evening social hour, which she invited the aides to attend, she played tapes of histories she had collected in other locations. During the performance, she recorded and played back an interview with one of the residents, and she asked the older people on the staff also to contribute. By obtaining the sanction of the staff members, she was able to complete her study.

In most cases, the field researcher will not be asked to show an identification card or produce a letter of reference. When the authorization is demanded, however, it must be instantly produced. Since the names and titles of distant officials may carry little authority in local settings, he should also have some local references. Many communities operate under the so-called Green River Ordinance. This regulation, first enacted early in the century in Wyoming, prohibits peddlers or solicitors from entering private property without invitation. It was first applied against the Fuller Brush Company, but the principle has been enthusiastically adopted by towns whose officials do not distinguish between door-to-door salesmen of aluminum siding and field researchers. Obtaining a certificate or license from the police chief might be necessary in these situations. Citizens who do not consider it necessary to call the police might still want to verify your identification with a community agency. You must provide the information to satisfy such inquiries. At the least, you will want to notify the police department or sheriff and list your project with the chamber of commerce, the Better Business Bureau, the attorney general, the public library, and other sources of information. The people you contact may have had unpleasant experiences with high-pressure sales techniques and criminals masquerading as field researchers. There is little you can do to combat the apprehension they may have besides emphasizing your legitimacy, seeking support from trusted community figures, and providing adequate reassuring information on your activities.

Information

You will begin your work by identifying the people and agencies who should be notified about your project and providing them with information about who you are and what you plan to do. The fact that you volunteer this information, however, is no assurance that anyone will listen. The recipients are most likely to read what you have given them or listen to what you say if you make the materials as attractive as possible, both in appearance and presentation. If you show up at the newspaper office with scrawled notes on the project crumpled in your pocket and samples of the study materials sprawling from a soggy brown paper bag, you may receive the publicity you

Communications, Information, and Authorization

seek but in a form you do not appreciate. An article on your study should appear on the city news or science pages, not in the feature column devoted to oddities spotted around town. Despite your best efforts to communicate details of your work to others, however, much of the information will be disseminated piecemeal in answer to questions you are asked. Subjects and community members will want to know, among other things, who you are, what you are going to do with the data you collect, how much you are paid, who supports the study, and whether they can get similar jobs. Answering the questions provides you with an opportunity to give the information you want known.

The appropriate medium for publicizing the study varies with the characteristics of the intended audience and the degree to which community individuals and organizations are to be associated with the research, as well as with your decision on how much information will be publicized. Information should be worded in terms that are understandable to the recipients and published where they are most likely to see it. You would not, for example, place an advertisement for subjects on welfare in the financial pages of a newspaper or publish a letter of endorsement from the coach of the local athletic team in the book review weekly. Posting a notice on the supermarket bulletin board may be the best approach to women you will find.

Support from prestigious groups usually generates favorable publicity. If your study will contribute to knowledge about the activities of the United Fund or a children's hospital, you will benefit from the halo these institutions wear. More controversial subjects present problems. Partisans welcome research that supports their prejudices and reject studies that call them into question. Since every controversy has strong support on each side, you may find yourself drawn into local conflicts. Circumstances like this enhance the value of support from an impartial institution. If you are able to say that your work is sponsored by a university or public agency, you may be protected from having to take sides.

49

Field Research

You can expect to be asked about the purpose of the study, and you can also expect occasional challenges to the answers. The rule to follow is simple. You do not lie to respondents or subjects, although the design of the study may demand that you do not tell them everything about it. In some research studies, for example, informing the subject of the purpose of the study would invalidate his or her response. Your position in these circumstances is to provide all of the information possible and also tell the inquirers why you cannot tell them more. In practice, it is not hard to do. The subject may ask "Why do I have to rate the importance of all these health services I never use?" or "What difference does it make whether I complain about overcharging or not?" The answer can be "We need to know what people in this town think are important health care facilities" or "We are interested in knowing how people respond to these situations." It is not necessary to tell the subjects that you are evaluating interest in establishing a mental care facility or investigating consumer fraud. Indeed, if the subjects knew what you wanted to find out, they would strain to provide the exact answers needed. Much of your caution in minimizing bias is directed at protecting the study from the misguided zeal of its subjects.

Issues of public relations enter into the information that is provided about the study. At the very least, you will prepare statements that are to be made public, and you will keep records of what you have said and to whom you have said it. Working in the field, you will interact with people who have little experience with research. They may assist you out of courtesy or because they expect to gain from their association with you, but they may be very unsure of precisely what you intend to do and what they have agreed to do with you. These expectations must be formally recorded. In gaining their permission to conduct the research, you will have explained the project, but the explanation may have been forgotten or misunderstood. When there is an assumption that some benefit to the subjects or the community will result from your work, it is essential that you spell out exactly what you hope to accomplish. For example:

Communications, Information, and Authorization

The planning department of a utility company decided to investigate community interest in the recreational use of a large wooded area adjoining an electrical transformer station. The planners suggested that a survey be conducted to assess the likelihood that people would make use of the area for passive recreation, congruent with the company's policy of minimal development of the vacant land. The company agreed that obtaining public opinion would be useful but objected to the cost of a special survey. Instead, a questionnaire included in the monthly billing statements asked customers whether they would make use of the area for picnicking or hiking and whether, as a local driving club had proposed, maintenance roads in the tract should be opened for use of all-terrain vehicles. Because the questionnaire was printed on a computer card, to save postage and processing time, no explanatory materials were provided. Inquiries about the questionnaire were answered by whatever receptionist happened to be on duty. No special briefing was provided, and each receptionist gave his or her own version of how the study was being conducted and what its purpose was. Based on this imprecise source of information, the environment reporter of the local newspaper wrote an article about the utility's plans; her account was contradicted almost completely in a feature story by the sports editor a few days later. The issue of preserving wilderness land versus allowing off-the-highway access to motorized vehicles was highly controversial at the time, and the argument exploded into the survey. Supporters of wilderness land attacked the utility for "giving away" the area to motorcyclists. Members of the local club leaped to the conclusion that the utility was prepared to accept their proposal and were very irritated when they were told that the company had not done so. The utility found itself in the position of having to justify its activities to both groups, and the resulting publicity made the survey useless. In this case, failure to make clear the purpose of the study and to explain what use would be made of the responses damaged the reputation of the sponsor, without providing it with the data it wanted. Given the sensitive nature of the subject, the study was almost certain to raise con-

51

troversy. Better information on what the researchers had attempted to do might not have salvaged the study, but it might have lessened the company's embarrassment. A separate mailing, with a full explanation of the purposes of the study and how the results would contribute to the decision-making process, would have been better.

Control of the information disseminated in your study also implies the ability to prevent unauthorized publicity. The most common sources of unwanted publicity are field staff members, to whom the study can provide interesting gossip about people and institutions they know. You will, of course, emphasize to the people you select that the information they obtain in the course of the research is privileged, but some spontaneous leaks are almost inevitable. Guarding against them is a constant problem. Less serious, but still troublesome, are the misstatements about the design and progress of the project which are casually made to the community. The weaker the contact you have with the field staff, the more likely is the exchange of misinformation among them. Providing both the staff and the public with accurate and up-to-date information permits you to remain in control of what is known.

Four

Staffing
the Project

◆◆◆◆◆◆◆◆◆◆◆◆◆◆◆◆◆◆◆◆◆◆◆◆◆◆◆◆◆◆◆◆◆◆◆◆

Research activities are carried out by people. Although you may decide to do all of the work yourself, researchers usually call on others to help. These people must often be recruited locally to assist the primary research team. The field staff must possess the skills that the tasks require, or else they must be amenable to appropriate training. In addition, they may sometimes be selected to meet a particular local qualification, such as race, language, or familiarity with community customs. Locally recruited staff members usually are untrained, naive about research, and in need of close supervision. They may see the project simply as a convenient way to earn a few dollars, or they may have such intense interest in the outcomes that their objectivity is suspect. In either case, they will require management. In contrast, people who have previously participated in research activities may be stubbornly set in techniques which do not meet your standards. Such people need to be retrained—which is sometimes more difficult than training the untrained. Assigning resources to recruiting, training, and supervision diverts them from other activities. Only in the unlikely case that there is more money available than can be easily used is the researcher free to spend extravagantly on field personnel. Under the usual circumstances, these costs, like all others, must be calculated carefully. Economical allocation of money for hiring and training field workers depends on cautious balancing of essential expenses against productivity. The first requirement is to determine exactly what is needed.

Assessing Staff Needs

The operations plan lists the tasks that must be done. Each of these tasks must now be translated into measures of expected effort, usually expressed as person/hours. Calculating person/hours is not difficult. It requires simply that the researcher define and record the actual work elements of the tasks and assign a specific time factor to each. For example:

As part of a study of the cost-effectiveness of part-time custodial workers, interviews were to be conducted with nursing supervisors at a large urban medical center. The pretest established that the interview would take from thirty to forty-five minutes, and appointments were set up at one-hour intervals. The hospital complex included several buildings, built and remodeled over many years. The nursing stations, where the interviews would take place, were separated by a variety of corridors, ramps, stairways, and courtyards, which did not always communicate directly with each other or the main entrances. The supervisors were busy, and their time could not be wasted.

The researcher had to decide how many interviewers to hire and how to schedule their work most efficiently. The pri-

mary calculation, of interview/hours, could be made immediately. Twenty-five interviews of up to forty-five minutes in
length would take slightly less than nineteen hours. One interviewer, working four hours per day, could complete these in a
week. But the interviewer also had to travel to the nursing station, finding his or her way through the complicated structures.
Traveling, even from one floor of a building to another, would
take time. In order to conduct an interview, the researcher
would have to meet with the respondent, answer questions,
accept or refuse an offer of coffee, and engage in some minimal
social interaction to put the subject at ease. These activities set
the stage for the research. Taking all this into account, the researcher had allowed a few minutes between interviews. Even
though the interviewer would not be collecting data during this
time, he or she could not do anything else, either, and would
probably expect to be paid for the time. The nineteen hours of
interview time, thus, could require twenty-five or more hours at
the site.

The interviewers would also have to edit the interview
responses, to make sure that answers were completely entered,
short notes properly amplified, and special abbreviations spelled
out and that dates, times, ID numbers, and so on were correct.
In order to benefit from immediate recall, the editing would
have to be done as soon as possible after the interview was
completed. Between appointments, then, or as soon as a day's
work was over, the interviewer would spend some time reviewing the protocols. This time, too, had to be added to the fieldwork schedule. Twenty-five hours on site could well have expanded to thirty or more by the time the work was ready for
delivery.

As a rough rule of thumb, many researchers estimate
fieldwork at one and a half to two times the data collection
period. The estimates vary, of course, with the tasks. Certain
time requirements, like certain money costs, are fixed. It takes
no longer to set up a display to be evaluated by two thousand
observers than one to be judged by fifty. If they all fill out a

rating form simultaneously, the larger number will use up no more of the researchers' time than the smaller group of spectators. How long it takes to collect rating forms, however, may be a function of the number of subjects. Rather than hours, it may be simpler for you to calculate in terms of some other work unit, such as a fixed number of observations or products. Your design, for example, might call for subjects to meet in groups of ten to taste-test and rate four new flavors of freeze-dried apricot dessert bars for inclusion in military survival-ration meal packets. Since each testing session will give you forty ratings, you might decide to use forty ratings as a work unit, rather than attempting to estimate the amount of staff time required to produce this result. Remember, however, that work units are also measures of time by people. If you plan to conduct the research by yourself, you must base the calculations on your own capabilities, with due acknowledgment of any limitations you may have.

Once the total number of hours or products required for a project is determined, this sum is divided by the number of hours or products that one person can be reasonably expected to accomplish during the period allotted to that part of the project. Thus, for the study on cost-effectiveness of part-time janitors, the researcher calculated as follows: 19 hours of interviewing plus 8 hours for organizing and setting up the interviews (staging time) plus 7 hours' editing equals 34 hours. For this study, the researcher had decided that the best interviewers would be nurses. Working part time, they could be expected to put in a maximum of fifteen hours overtime per week. A union contract negotiating deadline required that the data be collected within one week. The equation then became: 34 (needed hours) ÷ 15 (possible hours per week per person) = 2.3 people.

Since she wanted to err on the side of caution, the researcher hired three rather than two interviewers. These figures apply to a small and uncomplicated study. When larger numbers and more complex organizations are involved, the arithmetic becomes correspondingly more difficult. For example:

Staffing the Project

An Indian tribal council received a federal grant to conduct a complete survey of reservation resources. The study, which was to include an economic assessment of tribal land, housing and agricultural structures, educational and occupational qualifications of tribal members, and a complete demographic census of the tribe, was to be conducted, to as great an extent as possible, by tribal members, under the direction of a research staff employed by the tribe. Two main tasks were defined as follows:

1. *Property assessment:* On-site examination of housing stock; work buildings; agricultural, grazing, and forested land; and schools, clinics, and other public service structures.
2. *Household survey:* Interviews with representatives of all households, whether residing on the reservation or in other locations. Single individuals who did not maintain separate households would be interviewed independently.

The operations schedules for these tasks appear in Figures 4 and 5.

As director of this study, you estimated the work requirements as:

> *Property assessment:* 1,500 household units, at 3 hours each, including travel; and 85 public service structures, at 3 hours each. Data retrieval and archival research, at 1 hour per household unit.
>
> *Survey:* 2,000 individual and household interviews, at 1.5 hours each, plus 1 hour travel and .25 hours' editing per interview.
>
> *Scheduling, listing, and miscellaneous clerical:* Preparation of forms, 60 hours; correspondence, .5 hours per household; listing and scheduling, .25 hours per interview; general typing, 80 hours; records and payroll, 250 hours; transcribing field notes, 120 hours; reports, 80 hours.

Figure 4. Property Assessment Operations Plan

Subtask	Location	Staff	Materials	Time	Notes
1. Site location					
a. Identify locations, prepare maps	Tribal office, county records office, State Bureau of Land Use Management	Team, county land agent, rep. from Bureau of Indian Affairs, tribal business agent, Aerial Land Surveys, Inc., tribal police deputy, assistant tax assessor, and staff	Maps, tax rolls, plats, Treaty and Amendments (1872 ff), geological reports survey	Prior to Feb. 1 (coordinate w/State Land Hearing)	See Memo CL-3447, check court rulings in law library
b. Prepare sample assessment	Reservation	Team	Maps, measuring instrument, camera	Prior to Feb. 4	Have clean copy duplicated for training
2. Staffing					
a. Recruit	Tribal office, U.S. Employment Service, Haneville, Dry Fork Community College	Team, job counselor (EEOC), tribal business agent, interpreter	Job descriptions, maps	Feb. 1-5	
b. Hire	Tribal office	Team, tribal business agent	Employment forms, Social Security forms, brochures on insurance, tax forms, office supplies	Feb. 6-7	See if rep. from EEOC wants to sit in
3. Training					
a. Prepare training material	Office, reservation, printer	Team (reviewed by tribal officials, cartographer, draftsman)	Assessment of sample area	Prior to Feb. 6	

Task	Location	Personnel	Materials/Equipment	Date	Notes
b. Class	Tribal office Auditorium	Team, interpreter, rep. from Aerial Surveys, Inc.	Text, record forms, cameras, maps, films, measuring instruments	Feb. 12-16	
c. Field	Reservation (sample)	Team, drivers, trainees	Maps, forms, cameras, film, tape recorders, measuring instruments	Feb. 18-20	Depends on weather—road open?
4. Schedule and assignment (correspondence)	Project office (open Jan. 10)	Team, clerical staff	Office supplies, location charts, tally forms, etc.	Start Jan. 15	Coordinate w/interviews
5. Data collection					
a. Field	Reservation	Team, field staff	Forms, maps, instruments, vehicles	Start Feb. 21	
b. Archival	Project office, County Records Office, tribal office, museum	Team, clerical staff		Start Feb. 25	
6. Data entry					
a. Edit, verify	Project office	Clerical staff, team	Tally sheets, records, raw data	Start Feb. 28	
b. Reduce	Project office	Clerical, team	Key punch, cards, tape	Start Mar. 15	

Figure 5. Household Survey Operations Plan

Subtasks	Location	Staff	Materials	Time	Notes
1. Sampling					
a. Locate	Project office, tribal office, school district	Team, clerical staff, tribal health officer	Tax rolls, voter lists, school attendance lists, BIA records	Prior to Feb. 1	
b. List	Project office	Clerical staff	Office supplies	Prior to Feb. 15	
2. Instrument					
a. Develop	Project office	Team	Office supplies	Prior to Feb. 1	
b. Pretest	Reservation	Team, interpreter	Vehicles, tape recorder	Prior to Feb. 6	
c. Revision	Project office	Team		Feb. 10	
d. Printing	Haneville Press	Clerical staff		Feb. 18	Arrange delivery
3. Staffing					
a. Recruit	Tribal office, U.S. Employment Service, Haneville, Dry Fork Community College	Team, job counselor (EEOC), tribal business agent, interpreter	Job descriptions, maps	Feb. 1-5	
b. Hire	Tribal office	Team, tribal business agent	Employment forms, Social Security forms, brochures on insurance, tax forms, office supplies	Feb. 6-7	See if rep. from EEOC wants to sit in
4. Training					
a. Prepare	Project office	Team, clerical	Office supplies	Prior to Feb. 20	Start as soon as revision is done

	Location	Personnel	Materials	Dates	Notes
b. Class	Project office, tribal headquarters conference room	Team, interpreter	Instruments, manuals, practice materials	Prelim. Feb. 20; specific Feb. 22	
c. Practical	Reservation	Team, interpreter	Materials, vehicles	Feb. 22-24	
5. Assignment scheduling (correspondence)	Project office (open Jan. 10)	Team, clerical staff	Office supplies, location charts, tally forms, etc.	Start Jan. 15	Coordinate with property assessment
6. Data collection	Field staff, team, supervisors	Reservation	Instruments, vehicles	Start Feb. 25	
7. Data entry					
a. Edit	Project office	Supervisors, team		Start Feb. 26	Schedule retraining as needed
b. Verify	Project office, reservation	Supervisors, clerical	Vehicles	Start Feb. 26	
c. Reduce	Project office	Clerical, team		Start Feb. 26	
d. Enter	Project office	Clerical	Key punch	Start Mar. 1	Schedule access hours

Your figures, then, would have been:

> 6,255 (hours of property assessment) ÷ 40 (hours/week) = 156 person/weeks.
> 5,500 (hours of survey activities) ÷ 40 (hours/week) = 138 person/weeks.
> 1,715 (hours of clerical work) ÷ 40 (hours/week) = 43 person/weeks.

You reached these figures by a combined process of imagination and arithmetic. The operations schedule allowed you to count the number of necessary work units and to multiply each one by the amount of time you thought it would take, under normal circumstances. The basis for your decisions was experience, either your own or that of consultants, with similar work. Even though your project called for tasks that you had not directed before, they were likely to be made up of comparable subtasks. Typing a letter of given length takes a certain amount of time, irrespective of the content, and data gathering can be estimated in terms of similar activities under equivalent conditions. Where you must allot effort to unfamiliar tasks, you can easily experiment to find out or ask "How long does it take to weigh ten packets?" or "How many 95-item multiple-choice tests can one person score in an hour, under typical conditions?" It is even more useful to make these time estimates as part of the pretest you will conduct. Recording the exact time and cost expenditures of a pilot study will enable you to project them in the proper scale to the study as a whole. In making these estimates, you will strive for accuracy.

Imagination is equally important. At some point relatively early in your needs assessment, allow yourself the opportunity to fantasize disaster. For some researchers, this is an inescapable stage in the proceedings; if you are not by nature pessimistic, this is the time to play the role. For every element in your design, construct a scenario of failure. Imagine that the group leaders get lost trying to find the site, that an irrecon-

62

cilable quarrel breaks out between the field supervisor and her staff, that the cameraman fractures his wrist. What human resources will you need to solve these problems? What is the most effective balance between the costs of overinsurance and understaffing? The final calculations of how many people, at what level of competence, should be selected to meet the project's staffing requirements must include both your best estimate of need and a realistic assessment of the value of a practical surplus.

Qualifications

Each person/week can be visualized as an empty slot or cell in your design. Knowing the number of person/weeks the project requires, you can now begin to fill these slots with people. The staff members who are chosen, however, are not all interchangeable. Some will already have special skills or training which can be utilized, while others can profit from varying degrees of teaching. The specific tasks in the operations schedule will enable you to identify the needed skills and to suggest appropriate test measures for verifying the applicants' abilities. For example, someone hired to tally observations can be asked to pass a test in arithmetic, and observers might be required to demonstrate their abilities to see and distinguish between different events. A candidate whose voice is harsh and whose grammar is unreliable should not be selected to lead a discussion group. Your work might require knowledge of a particular language or familiarity with a local dialect.

Beyond skills, however, certain characteristics might be desirable or necessary for particular activities. Both laws and common sense demand that you do not discriminate on the grounds of race, religion, or sex, in hiring in general. There are instances, however, where selection on the basis of one of these factors might be justified. A woman, for example, could not act as a participant observer in a sex-specific society of men. There is evidence that some racial minority groups respond differentially to researchers of their own and other types; if you are working in such communities, therefore, race might be a valid selection criterion. On the Indian reservation in the previous example, traditional patterns of behavior limited the subjects on which younger people might question their elders. In this case, choosing only mature interviewers minimized loss of information. There are still other situations where less specific criteria can be invoked but where a researcher can unknowingly offend community mores. A basic rule is to work only with those people who will be welcomed by the subjects in the research setting.

Staff members' qualifications extend beyond their personal attributes to take in issues of behavior and appearance. These are sensitive subjects and must be handled with caution. You must distinguish between your personal preferences and what the study demands. A particular style of dress may impress you as vulgar or pretentious, but if it does not violate common standards you would be unwise to criticize it. Indeed, local field workers are probably more aware of what fits into the community than you are, so that their idea of what is appropriate may be more realistic than yours. Research, however, is more formal than its practitioners may recognize and cannot be conducted casually. Some researchers believe that their representatives should dress so as to appear slightly above the subject in socioeconomic status; the argument here is that the subject will be pleased and flattered to work with someone he or she would typically respect. Others stress the desirability of matching the subjects' expectations in dress and behavior, so that a researcher distributing questionnaires at a sales meeting should look and behave like a businessman, while a biologist measuring fish caught at a dock should act like a fisherman. This is particularly important when staff members are required to act as participants or to disguise their purposes. Unobtrusive observers must be unobtrusive in appearance and behavior, as well as in their manner of collecting data.

Underlying your decisions about appearance and behavior

Staffing the Project

should be two principles. One is that your requirements should not interfere with the work you ask staff members to do. They must be able to dress and behave in ways that facilitate their work. The more important principle is basic to field research. You and your staff should do as little as possible to impede or affect the processes you are attempting to study. How you look and how you act must be adapted to that end.

Selection Factors

Finding the people to conduct your research depends on what you have already learned about the numbers you need and the specific skills or characteristics they should have. Putting these elements together, however, is not completely straightforward, since special circumstances also have to be considered. Dealing with the factors sometimes becomes an exercise in reasoning, similar to a textbook problem in logic. For example:

In recruiting staff members for the Indian tribal economic assessment, the researchers were made aware of a number of facts that affected applicant qualifications. These included the following considerations:

1. Applicants from the two families that traditionally provided chiefs to the tribe expected to serve in supervisory positions over other members.
2. Few tribal members were bilingual. In general, the younger people spoke only English, while many elders, particularly in the more isolated areas, spoke only the tribal language. Almost all of the younger people who spoke the tribal language were women.
3. There was no written form of the tribal language.
4. Although most of the women could drive cars, the four-wheel-drive trucks which were necessary to get to the undeveloped edges of the reservation were usually driven by men.
5. The young women who possessed clerical skills were almost all still students in the community's high school.

Field Research

6. A substantial number of young men had migrated for employment to two large industrial centers in adjoining states. When they returned to the reservation for short periods, they spent most of their time hunting, fishing, or traveling to visit friends.
7. Aggressive efforts by missionaries had left many people highly suspicious of visitors, even when these were fellow tribal members.

Adaptation to these conditions affected decisions on hiring and work assignment. Some of these adjustments were relatively simple. The high school teacher of business subjects, for example, was happy to arrange released time for several students to perform clerical work on the project as part of their studies; other students could work part time after school hours if the project office were kept open in the evenings. Relying on part-time workers, however, meant almost doubling the number of employees to fulfill the estimated 43 person/weeks, with an associated increased burden on payroll and supervision tasks. One of the chief's relatives was well qualified to supervise a portion of the work. The other was less competent. Since she was respected by most of the people, however, a special position was created, in which she introduced and explained the study to various tribal groups. Her appointment thus was sufficiently prestigious to her and at the same time eased the acceptance of other staff members.

Where staff needs were weighted by the requirements for special skills, the adjustments were more complex. Since most of the applicants who spoke the tribal language were women, who did not drive the trucks necessary to reach the native-speaking residents, teams of two or more persons were formed to work in the more isolated areas. During their visits, they could share the property assessment and survey tasks to a considerable extent. The time needed for the two activities was not equal, however—a situation complicated by the fact that in most cases the property assessment could be carried out independent of the presence of the residents, while the survey might require repeated trips until an adult respondent was contacted. Thus, the number of person/weeks allocated to these activities had to be adjusted on almost a day-to-day basis. The original estimates served as minimum figures but did permit hiring and training of the core group. In this case, there were no firm time limits for the study, other than making allowances for holidays and seasonal work schedules. Finally, the absence of many of the men required that a separate staff be recruited to work in the industrial cities where they were employed.

Sources

The numbers of people you need to do your work, and their qualifications, interact with factors of availability. Once you know how many staff members you must hire, and what their qualifications should be, you have to locate them and convince them to work with you. You may seek them either among those with a special interest in your research or in the population at large. There are advantages to both choices. By its very nature, field research tends to be sporadic; and well-qualified researchers are capable of holding permanent jobs. People who can do your work competently, and who are not already doing equally demanding work for someone else, are not easy to find. They must be attracted to your project, either because it offers a better opportunity to work than they might otherwise have or because the research itself deals with a subject they care about. Traditionally, field projects have recruited students or housewives, who can participate in intermittent, part-time work. Unfortunately, serious students have a prior commitment to their studies. This flaw, from your point of view, means that class schedules, exams, term papers, and study take precedence over your work. The curve of student participation can be neatly plotted against the institution's calendar. When your field schedule can also be adjusted to reflect these events, you may obtain a staff whose research expectations coincide with yours.

In recent years, the pool of housewives has also shrunk. The well-educated, active woman who a few years ago would gladly have accepted part-time work for a month or so is much more likely now to hold a full-time job or to have returned to school. However, women still volunteer for charitable or public welfare services, for causes they support. They will participate in a research project that pays competitively, provides stimulating work, or offers them the opportunity to satisfy a personal or intellectual interest. Organizations that operate in the subject area of your investigation can encourage their members to assist you. In these cases, the organization serves as a reference for the applicant.

To some extent, the shortage of middle-aged, middle-class female recruits is alleviated by the increasing number of educated young people who have left the university but have not yet settled on any other permanent or semipermanent slot in society to fill. Staff members selected from this group prove to be intelligent, familiar with at least the concepts of scientific method, and free of family or social obligations that might limit their participation in the fieldwork. There are, however, some major disadvantages to seeking your field staff among this population. Applicants of this type tend to be relatively resistant to conventional social constraints. They may have spent years cultivating characteristics of the counterculture. Their appearance, language, and manners fit admirably into college communities; outside that environment they may be poorly accepted. An applicant who informs the recruiter that his long hair doesn't matter because he is willing to keep it tied up in a ponytail may not be sufficiently reassuring. When the content of the study is congenial with street and campus cultures, however, staff members who can combine counterculture behaviors with research skills are essential.

Studies that examine nontraditional phenomena call for staff members who exhibit the appropriate appearance. For example, a study of drug familiarity and use among public school students included the collection of data through questionnaires administered in class. Previous research in this area had been challenged on the ground that students would be inhibited from reporting by the setting and the presence of school administrators and teachers. To minimize this effect, the researcher decided to send teams of administrators into the classrooms, each team balanced to represent male and female, white and minority ethnic identity, and "straight" versus unconventional characteristics. Since the parent organization for the research was a major university, the researcher had a large pool of students and former students from which to draw people who met the complex requirements. Requests through the various minority student organizations, word-of-mouth advertising at campus and off-campus locations frequented by students and ex-students who still made the university the center of their activities, and similar informal and ad hoc recruiting techniques produced an adequate number of blacks, American Indians, whites, Chicanos, and Asians to staff the project. Since each school was to be visited by a team that matched, insofar as possible, the racial and ethnic distribution of the pupils, the scheduling was extremely complicated and depended on initiative, flexibility, and almost split-second timing on the part of the field staff. Scenarios like one that called for a car taking a black woman, a Chicano man, and a white woman from a particular school to stop at a crossroad and exchange personnel with another car, which held two American Indians and an Asian-American couple, before dropping off a Filipino woman at still a third location were common. The researcher learned through experience that a young woman could change her ragged jeans for a pants suit, braid and put up her hair, replace her makeup and dangling earrings, and emerge to fit a completely different role, while similar transformations were much more difficult for men. Members of the field staff taught her that sending a coastal Indian into a mountain reservation created more tension than the match of race compensated for, and that city-bred Puerto Ricans had problems communicating with the Mexican migrant laborers whose children attended the schools in the sample. Experienced researchers predicted disaster for the fieldwork.

Despite the complexities of staffing, the long distances over which plans and last-minute revisions had to be correlated, and the extremely informal administrative procedures, the study finished on time and within budget. The field staff—who had been chosen on the basis of race, language, and unconventionality—subordinated their personal preferences to meet the stringent standards of time, place, and behavior which the work enforced. They did not, however, change their life-styles completely. Their attachment to the straight world remained tenuous. When a replication of parts of the study was conducted, the researcher again sought her original field staff. Two had moved to a commune; several were living in Europe, South America, or Nepal; the majority had simply disappeared.

In the cases where the researcher has some connection with the community of potential staff members, or can seek recruits through mutually known individuals, the opportunities to make good choices increase. Recommendations from fellow investigators, people in the community who are familiar with and supportive of the research, or organizations which set high standards of public interest for their members usually produce qualified candidates. When you must start your search from the beginning among a population at large, you lack the convenience of relying on the judgments of others. You cannot trust that applicants who respond to your appeals are universally suitable. Research skills are sufficiently special as to be rare among those whom you might reach.

Working through newspaper advertisements or employment agencies calls for caution. In conducting surveys, in particular, you may be able to take advantage of the large pool of part-time interviewers available in most communities. They are likely to be women experienced in market research or in the polls commissioned by political candidates or service agencies. Their prior training should be investigated closely. While some survey organizations work to very high standards of scientific research, many others make few efforts to train their employees and accept slovenly results. You will want to inquire in detail about how these applicants were trained and supervised and how their work was evaluated. You may ask the organizations these questions, but you should not expect them to admit it if their procedures are poor. Asking the applicants themselves to describe the system in detail will provide better information and will enable you to assess their understanding of research quality control as well. In general, universities and research institutes maintain more rigorous standards than do commercial companies and are somewhat more willing to refer and recommend their interviewers to other investigators. Universities and colleges are also valuable sources for other types of staff members.

Where studies are commissioned by or take place within organizations, the sponsoring agency may be willing to donate staff time to the project. When you have specifically asked the agency to provide people with special skills, and when there is a clear understanding of their position in the research structure, these people can be a valuable addition. When sponsors offer to supply labor rather than money you have budgeted, however, awkward relationships may be created. People paid by someone else and temporarily assigned to your study may have difficulty in deciding whom they actually work for. Even worse, their usual supervisors may have equal difficulty in remembering that they are supposed to be doing something else. You must be able to control the efforts of the people who work on your study. Problems of authority may be added to the employees' bias in dealing with research data about their permanent work. These considerations suggest that donations of labor should be viewed cautiously.

There is a second issue here. Ask yourself whether a sponsor's willingness to donate staff time is in reality a reluctance to invest adequate resources in the project. It is easy for a manager to say "We'll have a couple of the guys in the motor pool deliver your films and show them." It is usually much less easy to convince the foreman that he must give up two of his drivers when *you* want them rather than when shipments are slow. A sponsor who approves of your activities in general but does not believe that they are as important as those of the organization may grudge you the support you need in specific instances. There is an element of insecurity in conducting research with staff members who may be withdrawn from your study by some other authority. When you have funds to hire your own staff, or can work with volunteers responsible to you alone, these momentary rejections need not trouble you. If the sponsor wishes to donate labor, and you can integrate these people into your project without threat to the objectivity of the research, it is wise to make sure that you have a clear agreement on who will participate, reporting to whom under what conditions. Writing down the understanding may seem needlessly formal, but it is essential. If disagreements occur, your whole project may be at risk.

Assuring Objectivity

The decision on whether to use members of the client group (people who are in some way associated with the sponsoring organization or who utilize the system under investigation) must be carefully considered. Obviously, the more knowledgeable a person is about your work, the less training and supervision he or she will require. "Knowledge of," however, often translates into "strong feelings about." Those who adopt partisan positions on an issue are likely to be uncomfortable with the detachment toward its outcomes which objective research demands. You are justified in questioning their ability to be fair. This is particularly true of people involved in action on social issues. Their dedication to the cause will often lead them to volunteer assistance, at the same time it influences their perception of the field. Biased results may occur accidentally, as well, when field researchers are so identified with the issue that the subject is affected by familiarity with the opinions of the investigator. For example:

72

Staffing the Project

A Citizens' Committee on Community Schools was interested in assessing the need for establishing a preschool as part of the city system. In pursuit of this goal, they decided to conduct a census of children in the 2- to 4-year age range, to survey employers and women's groups on the predicted economic effects of providing preschool services, and to study the potential of present school facilities for expansion. Community opinion was sharply divided on the question. The Citizens' Committee strongly supported the proposal, while several conservative churches rejected the idea. The school board was not authorized to spend money on activities outside its area of operations, but the Teachers' Service League and the Good Neighbors Club of a major local industry offered to help. The Public Facilities Planning Office of the city agreed to contribute the efforts of a half-time community planner to direct the studies. An immediate problem that the planner faced was the necessity of obtaining a research staff. There was no money to hire professionals, and legitimate questions could be raised about the objectivity of volunteers from the Citizens' Committee or the National Organization for Women's Task Force on Child Care, which had already publicly advocated the program, or the Ladies' Christian Service Guild, which had placed advertisements in the newspapers denouncing the "ungodly" plan as a threat to family life. There were, however, two approaches that the planner could try. He could search for other volunteers, who might be less committed to a particular position; or he could redefine the task.

In this instance, both approaches were tried. Two separate categories of tasks were identified: those for which specific objective criteria could be developed and those vulnerable to subjective interpretation. The school census and the evaluation of facilities were of the first type, while the results of an opinion survey and the summary and report of the studies were more open to charges of misinterpretation. Appeals to two well-respected and impartial groups, the League of Women Voters and the American Association of University Women, produced the names of several members who were willing to conduct the opinion survey. The church women who opposed the preschool and some of those from among its proponents were asked to carry out the census. Almost everyone in the community supported this objective as an aid to planning. Since the school board's planning unit would derive an immediate benefit from the census, a small sum of money was made available to underwrite this part of the study. Technically qualified engineers from the Good Neighbors Club evaluated the facilities, and the industry, as a gesture of good will, volunteered its computer to analyze the data. The report was written by the planner.

Hired employees, of course, are easier to control than volunteers, but they are no less likely to have their own opinions. The factors that encourage them to participate in your study are the same as those that attracted their interest to the research in the first place. To some extent, this is desirable. Staff members who have no interest in your research other than as the source of their paychecks have little incentive to do well. The ideal situation is one in which they have a commitment to the research itself but not to its outcome. This combination is rare in the general population. It can frequently be found in students, which is a strong argument in favor of selecting them. Failing this, you must work to convince your staff that your inquiry into their prejudices and beliefs is a valid concern.

Applicants who are informed in detail about the purposes and design of the study have a good basis for understanding why you must ask certain questions and why their appointment may legitimately depend on their answers. The underlying concepts of scientific method, which provide the rationale for research activities, are not difficult to explain in lay language. Whether as volunteers or as employees, people who wish to work with you deserve a reasonable explanation for your decisions on their selection. When someone must be rejected because you believe that he or she will find it difficult or impossible to act impartially, it is important that the applicant knows why. You must explain that partisans are not at fault in hoping for one outcome over another but that the study must be guarded against their wishes' affecting the results. Given the opportunity, applicants will often select themselves out of certain aspects of the project and limit themselves to activities in which they feel comfortable. Adapting to these choices allows you to use individuals in some tasks who would not be suitable for participation in others, with satisfaction to you both.

Recruiting Methods

You may appeal for staff members either by word of mouth, through some formal advertising or agency procedure, or by a combination of methods. There are many advantages to securing new staff members through the grapevine. Recommendations from present workers imply that two desirable events— both good omens for employment—have occurred: The present staff member has explained what the job entails, and the applicant has been favorably impressed by the description. However, if the present workers' assumptions about job requirements and qualifications are wrong, and the applicant fails, you may also lose the friend or relative who is already working. Referrals from other researchers or coworkers can be highly productive. Applicants from such sources may be skilled, experienced, and sophisticated in research procedures. Although a scientist or manager might fulsomely recommend someone for the purpose of getting rid of him or her, most of your professional friends and acquaintances are more honorable. Where they cannot help you, they will be quick to suggest other agencies that might. Even when you are not personally connected with other research agencies, telephone calls or letters to universities or institutes can admit you into the research network where help is available.

Advertising can tap a larger pool. Depending on the needs of your work, you may wish to announce your positions either to the community at large or to some limited segment of the population. Job listings at employment agencies, newspaper ads, posters, or radio or television spots have the potential of attracting large numbers of applicants, most of whom will not meet your standards. It is an unfortunate fact of recruiting that the best-qualified employees are probably already working for someone else. Basing your selection on the responses to a mass appeal, you might expect to interview five to ten people for every one you accept and to accept two for every one who in turn accepts and succeeds in your position. When sizable numbers of people are to be chosen, the costs of screening can be considerable. You can minimize these costs by more selective recruiting, based on the characteristics of the subject population. Thus, a study of sports activities might be staffed by people recruited at athletic facilities, sports equipment shops, or classes, while signs posted at art museums and ads inserted in music and drama journals could attract the attention of people with an interest in surveying arts patrons. Even in isolated areas, it will be possible to find people who have some connection with the subject of the study taking place in their vicinity. You may be fortunate enough to find that the very isolation of the site results in a captive population. For example, research on military installations can usually draw on the large number of wives and other dependents living in on-base housing. Because of the lack of competing opportunities and the distance from urban areas, a request for applicants is seen as an exciting chance for work, which these people would not have anywhere else. The large numbers of families allow you ample choice of highly qualified candidates, while their familiarity with both the base and its inhabitants lessens difficulties of training and management. Even where there are few people, as in rural, mountainous, or desert areas, it is possible to locate enthusiastic staff members: a retired teacher or navy officer or the wife of a forester or state policeman. There are not many such people in any one place, but to them you may represent the sole chance to participate in an intellectually stimulating activity. The benefits you confer on each other are mutual.

Once you have arranged to notify people about the project, it is necessary to set up a system to respond to their inquiries, assess their capabilities, and accept or reject them. You may meet with applicants individually or in groups, provide them with applications, test their abilities, ask them to undergo some examination process, or discuss with them the extent to which they wish to become involved in the work. Usually you, and they, will go through several of these procedures, depending on their qualifications and your needs. At the very least, you must find out who the applicant is, what he or she can contribute to the task, and whether your terms are acceptable. How to do this depends on where, and under what conditions, field staff members are recruited. Some ways in which this first contact can be made are shown in the following examples.

Sixty field investigators to monitor traffic in seaside communities during the vacation season were needed for a study of the environmental impact of banning roadside businesses along a scenic highway. The researchers, from a city several hundred miles away, decided to recruit the field staff from small towns in the region. Ads in local newspapers; posters in libraries, colleges, and other public places; and listings at employment agencies requested those interested to apply after 10:00 a.m. on a certain day, at a given location in each of the towns. At the same time, a press release was sent to each of the newspapers, describing the study in general terms and mentioning that a field staff was to be hired. Because the researchers were coming to the town only for recruiting, there was no office. Reservations at a centrally located motel, however, assured that the applicants would know where to come and that telephone messages could be taken. Two team members came to each town; they checked into the motel early in the day, posted a notice in the lobby, and informed the desk clerk that applicants were to be sent to their rooms. Folding chairs and a stack of applications were placed outside the doors, and a sign was posted that instructed applicants to fill out the forms and wait in the parking area outside the building for their turn to meet with the recruiters.

Field Research

The first applicants arrived before 9:30. For the rest of the day, others came in a steady stream. A team member spent about ten minutes with each one (reviewing the application form, asking about the applicant's special qualifications, and explaining the study); at times, five or more people were waiting in line outside the rooms. By evening, more than a hundred people had applied. Some of these, of course, were obviously unfitted for the work, because of physical condition, available time, or inability to understand and utilize the instruments the study required. A number had come to investigate the job and, after learning about it, had decided that they were not interested. About fifty applications remained, of people whom the researchers wished to consider seriously. Immediately after interviewing each applicant, the team member had noted a score of 1 to 10 and brief comments on the application, such as "Seems very shy," "Says she has had a lot of statistical training," or "Very pleasant voice, has worked as receptionist." At the end of the day, the two researchers were ready to review the applications. Starting with those scored highest, and working down, they discussed each applicant, with the one who had interviewed that person commenting on the notes. Together, the team members decided on twelve applicants, who were to be invited to attend a training program. The work estimate for that community was for nine or ten people; the twelve chosen would allow for any who dropped out of the program or did not pass the training. By 9:00 the next morning, the researchers had made calls to notify the twelve who had been chosen and were on their way to the next town.

For another study, the researchers sought a small group to conduct sight and hearing tests of first- through third-grade children in a nearby city. Although the field staff would not need previous training, the ability to work with small children was important, as was accuracy in reading gauges and sensitive measuring devices. For political reasons, the researchers decided to choose only people living in the school district involved. Because only a small number of highly selected applicants were needed, mass recruiting was not conducted. Instead, announcements through parent groups, newspaper articles, and the newsletters of several service organizations requested interested people to call a listed telephone number, which was connected to an automatic answering device. Callers were asked to leave their telephone numbers and names. At intervals, the tapes of these calls were picked up by a researcher, who telephoned each of the callers to describe the study and obtain information on the applicants' qualifications. Those who appeared suitable were mailed a more detailed application questionnaire to be completed and returned. Final selection was made on the basis of these questionnaires, augmented by further telephone conversations when necessary. By the time the research team opened its field office in the city, a full staff had been recruited and were ready to begin the project.

For a third study, it was necessary to locate a number of black interviewers who were familiar with the inner city. The research team, part of a large commercial organization, had few contacts in the minority community and little credibility among those who had previously worked in the area. In this instance, they decided to recruit indirectly, through a federally funded inner-city job preparation program. The staff members of the program were invited to the corporation's headquarters for a meeting in which the study was explained and the qualifications for the interviewer candidates were specified. The program members made up a list from among their trainees and graduates, screened them for eligibility and skills, and scheduled appointments for them with the research staff. The researchers spent a day at the program's offices, meeting and evaluating the candidates. From them, the necessary number of interviewers were chosen. During the course of the study, the research supervisors were requested to make regular reports to the program on the interviewers' progress. In turn, program counselors were available to work with interviewers who failed to maintain productivity or had other work-related difficulties.

Each of these three examples displays a different combination of the researcher's effort, exploitation of the potential pool of applicants, and control over the selection process. Which you choose depends on your estimation of the relative advantages and costs of each of the factors, tempered by an accurate evaluation of the realities of the situation. Where the characteristics you desire are evenly dispersed over a wide population, and you have ample time to spend in the field, the sort of mass appeal and screening described first can be very effective. The second example is far more economical of your time but substantially narrows the range of people who will work through the multiple screens which you set up. If you are looking for a small number of applicants with relatively rare skills, you may find a variant of this method most useful. Finally, you may choose to give up much of your control over the selection of your staff in exchange for freedom from the necessity of devoting more than minimal time to the task. Like any other transaction, the methods you use for recruiting have costs and benefits. The decision should be based on what you are willing to give for the best product you can obtain.

Five

Field Staff
Management

◆◆◆◆◆◆◆◆◆◆◆◆◆◆◆◆◆◆◆◆◆◆◆◆◆◆◆◆◆◆◆◆◆◆

Even before you have com-
pleted the selection of your field staff, you should turn to the
questions of how they will be officially enrolled in the project,
what and how they will be paid, how they will be trained, and
who will supervise them. If your field study is small, relatively
simple, and under your complete control, and if whatever funding it requires is personally accountable by you, very informal
arrangements can be made. A study of this type might be one in
which only you and your colleagues will carry out the fieldwork, assisted by your spouses. No special supplies or materials
are needed, beyond those already available in your office. Your
only expenditures will be for gas and meals, refundable through
an in-office voucher. Since the time you spend on the project is

part of your regular work time, you need not worry about insurance, Social Security contributions, sick leave, or vacation increments, and you are responsible for the welfare of your spouses. For most field research, however, formal procedures for hiring, training, and supervising are specified by the parent organization, established by tradition, or especially designed to meet the needs of a project.

Hiring

Field workers usually become part of the staff of the parent organization. This means that they must be formally hired at the beginning and their positions terminated at the end of the project, by whatever procedure the organization has established. They may be required to join a union, enroll in pension or health insurance plans, and undergo medical examinations or security investigations. In many instances, the researcher will have to convince the organization that new people, with qualifications that do not fit neatly into existing job descriptions, must be chosen, sometimes in violation of requirements for seniority preference or notification procedures. Most large organizations make some provision for employing intermittent or part-time staff, but personnel offices usually attempt to keep these appointments to a minimum—largely because they require more paperwork than usual. One researcher remembers a long and acrimonious correspondence with a university's personnel office, in which she attempted to explain why her request for twelve field staff members to work for eight weeks could not be satisfied by the creation of new staff positions for two people on a yearly basis.

When large numbers of new and short-term appointments must be processed through a procedure set up to handle another type of activity, the sheer quantity of paper generated can create a problem in itself. You must, therefore, arrange to do as much of this work as possible in advance. Learn the capabilities and limits of the system you must use; knowing that appointments for requisite medical examinations are scheduled two weeks ahead, for example, permits you to block out the time for your new employees before they are hired. Later, you can fit their individual appointments into the hours you have claimed. Most bureaucracies are highly resistant to change and suspicious of anyone who attempts to bypass or force their mechanisms; but they are also usually made up of reasonable individuals, who are quite amenable to discussing with you the most efficient ways of utilizing their machinery for your needs. Establishing a connection, and finding out what procedures to use before the fact, can solve many problems. Once you have successfully maneuvered your way through a complex system, you should document your steps, so that you can use them again in similar situations.

It is sometimes possible to hire field staff members in a simpler way. They may be named as consultants, to provide some special services on a limited basis, or as contractors or suppliers, to sell their services for some specific task. In these cases, the individuals usually do not become employees of the organization and are not included in its program of benefits. Their taxes, insurance, and pensions are their own responsibility, and they typically receive payment in a lump sum at the end of the project, rather than salary checks on some regular schedule. To some people, work under these conditions is preferable. Volunteers may not be paid at all.

Not paying your staff members, however, does not completely release you from paperwork surrounding their appointments. At the very least, you will need to list their names, record their qualifications, and make explicit their responsibilities. They will need as much training as paid employees do, and frequently they will require even more elaborate supervisory structures—particularly when they are acting under some sort of personal obligation to you as an individual. If they are your students, friends, or family members, directing their activities and enforcing standards of quality are likely to be complicated by their feelings about you and yours about them. Another complication is the fact that those who participate out of a sense of commitment to an issue may develop strong feelings of proprietorship about their cause. If your research interests are different from theirs, cooperation may falter. Communication with volunteers should be amply documented and systematically recorded.

To an increasing extent, even volunteers come under organizational constraints and protections. Your project may be required to carry insurance for its volunteers and to document that they fall within guidelines for fair employment or meet other institutional criteria for selection. Since, to a very real extent, you become responsible for the actions of your staff members in the field, procedures which assure you that their actions will not leave you liable are as essential for volunteers as they are for employees. You must make sure that all the people who will work on your project have a clear understanding of their rights and responsibilities.

What your staff members know about their position should come from you, rather than as gossip from other workers. At the very least, you must inform them as soon as possible after selection that they have been appointed and when they can be expected to begin work. To avoid misunderstandings, details on what their responsibilities will be, how much they will earn, how long the project will last, and under whose direction they will work should also be provided in writing. In the typical fieldwork situation, where staff members have little direct contact with the parent organization, the information you supply may be all they ever know about their employer. Misunderstandings about pay rates, hours of work, benefits, and responsibilities are common, particularly under the fluid conditions characteristic of much field research. Staff members will receive much of this information during their training, but they should have it in written form before this time. Appropriate details for volunteers, contractors, or consultants are similarly important. Indeed, such information is even more necessary when staff members will not be regular employees. Institutions usually provide their employees with brochures and formal orientation materials that are not available to new staff members under other arrangements.

Although you are not required to communicate with unsuccessful applicants, doing so is a courteous and useful gesture. Those who have applied deserve to have their uncertainty satisfied by a definite answer, even if it is a disappointing one. Remember that these people are probably members of the community in which you will work. Their services may not be necessary to you, but their goodwill is.

Pay Rates and Working Conditions

Money, esteem, intellectual and personal stimulation, and pleasant working conditions are the tokens you will exchange for the efforts of the staff members. It is to your advantage, if you want to attract and hold the best people, to make the rewards as high as possible within the limits of the budget and the physical necessities of the project. You will be in competition with other employers for personnel. What you must offer varies with factors such as the availability of other employment, cost-of-living figures, the nonmonetary rewards of the study, and the cost of the work to the applicant, in discomfort or inconvenience.

By its very nature, field research can be uncomfortable and sometimes even dangerous for its practitioners. People who are not acclimated to outdoor work may be called on to stand for hours on street corners, walk long distances, or jostle their way through crowds. They must be prepared to adapt quickly to unusual situations and bizarre time schedules and to maintain their own behaviors under such control that they can move without overt disturbance into unexpected circumstances. In many cases, there is little you can do to help them. Efforts to modify the environment for the convenience of the researchers are likely to contaminate the field under study. You can recommend rubber boots and warm clothes, suggest the wording of appropriate introductory formulas that may gain them access to shelter, point out the location of coffee shops and toilets, and make sure that they have the flashlight, road map, building key, extra supplies, and personal safety equipment they are likely to need; but in reality field workers must be responsible for themselves. In fact, they may be far more familiar than you are with the necessities for operating safely and efficiently in their home areas. When a local resident tells you that county clerks are usually on duty a half hour before the official opening hour, or that during rainstorms a particular community can be reached only by a certain back road, it is wise to listen. His familiarity with local conditions is one of the most important contributions he will make.

As the manager of a field research project, you will be expected to assume the ultimate responsibility for the conditions under which the work is done. In field research, you quickly become aware that your ability to affect the world is limited. By yourself, you cannot provide your staff with comfortable office furniture, quiet and well-lighted surroundings, and pleasant companions. When these are found in the field, it is a fortunate but fortuitous occurrence. What you can do is to learn the field conditions and insert into them the maximum convenience for your staff. For example, you can inspect the hospital wards as well as reach an agreement with the supervisor on where your interviewers will work; or, you can check the bus schedule instead of accepting the park superintendent's assertion that "It's easy to get back to town after the game." The constraints of the research may offer you little scope. Building an elaborate weatherproof booth for your observers may make them more comfortable but will handicap them in their tasks of weighing the trash discarded at wilderness camp sites. Instead, you and they may have to be satisfied with sturdy rain gear and plastic covers for their supplies. You would not be excused from at least making sure that, somewhere, they have access to a stove for drying their socks. Beyond this you may be helpless.

You can, however, make a significant impact in the area

of protecting your field staff from the inconveniences of working in your own organization. Systems are set up to serve the needs of the organization. Regular, permanent employees of the organization benefit from, or at least learn to adapt to, their system; they plan their weekends, budget expenditures, and schedule their trips to and from work to fit their knowledge of when they will be paid, how early they can leave the office for a special event, or how far in advance their vacation must be planned. Such knowledge comes with experience; part-time or intermittent staff members may never learn it, or may learn it too late. Field workers are often only marginally associated with conventional employment; their demands on the system may be greater at the same time that their understanding of it is less. There will be many occasions when you will have to intervene to meet the needs of your staff.

A frequent difficulty involves the timing of pay. Payroll cycles often operate on a monthly basis, so that new employees hired on May 10, for example, will not receive their first check until June 30. Permanent staff members must adjust to this situation, but only once. After their first check is delivered, they can plan their expenditures with some degree of reliability. With the irregular employment typical of field research, a staff member may work a few days, wait six weeks to be paid, and then reenter the cycle at some different point. If your field staff can be enrolled as consultants or suppliers, their burden may be eased, although the managers of the system are unlikely to approve. All systems, however, have some point at which they are vulnerable to intervention. Learn what the peculiar bypass procedure is for your system and provide yourself in advance with whatever is needed to operate it. Remember that events in the field tend to be fleeting. The system has more time to adapt than your project has.

Applicants may be attracted by the challenge of difficult work as much as by the salary they are offered. Staff members you hire will receive money, but they will also expect personal satisfactions. Volunteers expect to gain even greater personal rewards from participation in your project. The satisfactions they receive from contributing to a cause they value are of most importance to them. But both volunteers and employees must understand the significance of the research, and accept it as a valid endeavor, if they are to be retained. Local people, recruited ad hoc to work on short-term projects, lack many of the attachments to the activity which permanent staff members develop. It is difficult to maintain their interest. Frequent rewards —in the form of complimentary reviews, progress reports, and personal interactions between the field staff and the research team—serve this purpose. The quality and intensity of supervision are especially important.

Supervision

Full-time, permanent employees of an organization usually understand and adapt to the system's hierarchy. The jerry-built staff structures typical of field research rarely provide this secure an environment. Field staff members must work out for themselves the correct patterns of interaction. Particularly when the supervisors as well as those supervised are drawn from the same population, it is sometimes difficult to explain to everyone's satisfaction why Mrs. Jones, with two years of college and some clerical experience, is selected to direct a field team, while her next-door neighbor, Mrs. Smith, with similar qualifications, is not. There is no easy way to reconcile such issues. Whenever possible, therefore, you should try to assign all supervisory responsibility to staff from the parent organization. When this cannot be done, make the reasons for your choices clear and justifiable.

Bringing in a supervisor from the outside, however, also creates some special problems. Field workers who are members of the same community share a basis of personal association. They will meet at church or the supermarket to exchange information and chat about subjects of interest. When they are staff members of your project, their conversations will also include discussions about their work and advice on problems raised by the research. They may be more comfortable asking for help from a friend than from the stranger who is their supervisor. This type of informal training and interpretation may include a considerable amount of error. In any event, since you will not wish to give up authority, you will need to control participant supervision. You can do so in several ways. In training, emphasize the necessity of referring questions directly to the supervisor. The implication of this direction is that the supervisor must be available to answer. Provide field staff with addresses or telephone numbers where they can find assistance. This is particularly important when the work will be done outside of usual office hours; it does very little good to offer a telephone referral number staffed from 8:00 to 5:00 on Monday through Friday if the emergencies are most likely to occur on Tuesdays at midnight or on Sunday mornings. Since most supervisors will not guarantee twenty-four-hour availability on every day of the week, it is advisable to provide more than one possible source of assistance, such as a local workday office, an evening and weekend home telephone, and, in cases of urgency, a way of reaching the principal investigator or parent organization.

In addition to making themselves available, supervisors must also make interactions with staff as stress free as possible. You assume that your field workers will carry out routine assignments competently. They usually will not contact you unexpectedly while things are going well. The telephone call at 6:00 a.m. or the hurried trip to your home, then, is a sign of trouble. The caller already knows that something is wrong. A field worker who asks for help may already be under great tension; scolding or harsh criticism may produce panic. Dealing with an emergency calmly and patiently can often retrieve what appears to be a disaster. You can always retrain, chastise, or fire the staff members later, under cooler conditions. Field workers who learn to trust their supervisors will not be afraid to ask for help, often before things get seriously out of order. Trust and familiarity are built up out of frequent and rewarding contact.

89

Field Research

The supervisor should communicate with staff members on a regular basis, asking about progress in a friendly way, checking to make sure that the workers' supplies are adequate, and providing feedback on what has been submitted. It is less threatening to admit having problems to a supervisor who calls several times a week to ask "How are things going? Did the trouble with your car get fixed? What can we do to help you?" than to a scarcely known figure who calls only to correct mistakes. Finally, staff members must be informed of changes and new interpretations of study materials. The supervisor should be sure that instructions are updated to account for the almost inevitable modifications which will be made. A weekly memo to all field workers, for instance, can inform them of new procedures, provide rewarding details about the progress of the study, and enhance their feeling of membership in the research endeavor. (See Chapter Eight.)

Friends and Relatives

Relying on the efforts of a field staff composed of friends and/or relatives presents a special case of management technique. Maintaining personal relationships within the designated control procedures ideally requires meticulous selection, tactful supervision, and the ability to divorce work relationships from intimate interactions. Unfortunately, personal associates are usually selected not because they are the best qualified but simply because they are available. The researcher may have no choice but to recruit them, and they may accept, not out of interest in the project but rather from a sense of obligation or affection. A family or friendship research enterprise can be successful when the team clearly consists of a single principal researcher and one or more assistants, when the lines of authority are clear, and when there is agreement on the scope of the work and the standards that must be met. The traditional model of a field project operated through personal motivation is that of the researcher who asks his or her spouse to help out in data collection activities. The assumption in such situations is that both researchers share a desire to complete the work, an understanding of what that work entails, and common expectations of its rewards.

Setting up and managing a system of this sort requires careful planning and informed commitment on the part of all the members. Even then, the primary investigator will be limited to some extent in the demands that can be made and in the sanctions that can be applied. For example, an elementary school teacher held a summer job as supervisor of playground activities in a large city park. He was also enrolled as a part-time student in a graduate program in educational psychology and had reached the point of conducting research toward his doctorate. He proposed a study on the relationship of coaching style to the success of Little League baseball teams in a sample of first-year players and their parent coaches. The field aspects of the study required observing and scoring the behaviors of coaches on three diamonds over a six-week season. Since play on the three fields was simultaneous, the teacher had to recruit observers to assist him. His wife was the obvious first choice. Herself a teacher who had completed her graduate work, she was sympathetic to the project, knowledgeable about baseball, and able to accompany her husband to the park each day. The couple were willing to devote every day of the study period to data collection. Finding others equally dedicated was not easy. Games were scheduled on each diamond an average of four evenings a week, for a total of twenty-four games over the season. Assigning an observer to the third baseball field required scheduling a number of people to rotate over the days and weeks of the study. The researcher estimated that two observers would be needed to fill the slots each week; he therefore recruited his brother, a college athlete, and a sports-loving friend who volunteered. The researcher trained the observers in the use of the scoring forms he had developed, and the study began. Almost immediately, difficulties arose. The friend informed the researcher that he planned to take a vacation before the end of

91

the summer and would not be available for the second week of the study. A frantic search for another volunteer among the couple's friends was unsuccessful, but the wife mentioned the problem in explaining their failure to attend a family picnic, and her elderly aunt offered to help. After a crash course in baseball, she was qualified to take over the observer's post on the third diamond. Meanwhile, a disagreement occurred between the researcher and his brother, who had taken a course in coaching. The brother chose to interpret the coach's behaviors in terms of his own knowledge and refused to use the scoring system which had been established. After several quarrels, and increasing bad feeling between the two, the brother quit. Fortunately, this coincided with the return of the friend, and the wife's aunt could now be asked to take over the vacant post. She agreed reluctantly, citing her preference for keeping up her garden in the evenings. Desperate, the researcher's wife volunteered to do the gardening in the mornings, although she was aware from experience that her skill would not meet her aunt's rigidly high standards. The researcher, in equity, took over the housework his wife had previously done. He also felt obligated to join his friend in attending several other sporting events, which did not especially interest him. By the end of the summer, the data collection was complete, at the cost of considerable effort and strained family relations. Given the limited financial resources of the researcher, there were few alternatives, but the fieldwork was not cheap in human terms.

Training

Careful selection procedures, adequate rewards, and competent supervision will do much to maintain the quality of your fieldwork. Even willing, well-qualified staff members under the direction of skilled supervisors, however, must first learn what they are supposed to do. The training they receive must be planned and carried out in meticulous detail.

The amount and intensity of the training the field staff

receives depend on the complexity of the tasks, the skills which they possess, and the degree to which they will be required to work independently, without the immediate supervision and assistance of the researchers. Almost by definition, fieldwork takes place away from the organization's central location, under varying conditions of isolation. Preparing the field staff to operate efficiently and productively in these circumstances is the goal of the training program that will be conducted.

Training materials should be written for each element of the study. The field staff must have some available reference in hand, and that reference must include information on how to solve every problem they are likely to meet. Whether you also provide instructions on coping with the unlikely situations is a question you must decide for yourself. There are arguments in favor of supplying directions for even the most bizarre situation, and equally convincing arguments against frightening new staff members by gruesome renditions of their predecessors' sufferings, even if these ended in triumph. Which course you choose depends on your estimation of how frequently the traumatic situations will occur, how demanding they are, and how competent your trainees appear to be.

The materials should contain step-by-step instructions for doing what you want done, sufficient background information to answer both the staff members' questions and those which the public might ask, and clear definitions of every term and concept with which the research will deal. Even such simple terms as *ask, record, complete,* or *continue* may have special meanings when applied to your project; relying on your understanding of the trainees' interpretation may be insufficient. It is still more important to specify less common concepts. In addition to the definitions and instructions, the training should include examples, illustrations, and supervised practice, to make sure that the trainees understand how to apply your instructions.

If you will not train all your staff members personally,

you must also train those who will undertake this responsibility. In allowing others to do this work, you are losing some of your control over how it is done. You must, therefore, take steps to assure that your standards will be met by the instructors who are assigned to the job. Your research associates may do the training, in which case you can probably assume that they share your interest in what the training provides and how. The further from your project you must reach to obtain the skills you need, the more effort you must expend to monitor the training process. No one else knows or cares as much as you do about the quality of the preparation which your staff carries into the field. It is possible, however, that your particular expertise extends only to the content and not necessarily to the methods of training. If you have chosen a professional or experienced trainer, you are well advised to allow him or her to work without interference. You will probably attend the training meetings, but your contribution should be offered before the meeting starts, rather than interjected into the process. Students are confused and alienated by dissension among their instructors. The agenda should be set, the topics selected, and the required level of performance determined before the trainees enter the room.

What you will teach and how you will teach it depends on the work to be done. Trainees should learn what tasks they will do, how to do them successfully, and how to cope with the conditions they will experience. The instruction should be both theoretical and practical, with the candidates given the opportunity to test themselves, ask questions, and try out the suggestions they are given. Class or individual teaching should be followed by practice under both simulated and real field conditions. See Figure 6 for an example of what the materials for a training session might be and Figure 7 for a sample training agenda. For the trainers, each item on the agenda must be expanded to include the information it will cover, the materials which will be needed for that phase of the project, and indication of how it will be taught.

Field Staff Management

Figure 6. Sample of Training Materials

Western County Fire District 103
First-Aid Course Evaluation
Field Staff Training Meeting—November 6, 1978

Background

Western County Fire District 103 has received a grant from the State Department of Public Health to evaluate the first-aid programs offered by a number of fire districts, school systems, and public safety divisions in Western and Newburg Counties. In addition to other studies, public first-aid classes offered in November will be monitored to determine the numbers and experiences of those attending, the topics covered, the specific audiovisual materials utilized, and the extent to which members of the public at the meetings recall the materials presented.

Tasks

Staff members will be assigned to the following tasks during the course of the study:

- Applicants and attendees tally
- Class topics recording
- Audiovisual materials recording
- Evaluation of the class
- Skill assessment survey

These tasks are described as follows:

1. *Applicants and attendees tally.* Each organization which conducts first-aid training will provide us with the advance registration list for the course. The staff member will have this list of names, in alphabetical order, before he or she gets to the class. As each person who attends signs in, the staff member will check his or her name off and will verify the address.

2. *Class topics recording.* Researchers will note each topic covered by the instructor. With the stop watch which you will receive, you will record the number of minutes allotted to each topic and the number of minutes for each type of class activity, such as lecture, discussion, quizzing, practice. The topics and times for each activity will be entered on the class record sheets you will have for each class.

3. *Audiovisual materials recording.* During the class, you will record the types of audiovisual instructional materials used, and the times for each, on the record sheet. Either during the class or at its end, you will note the exact name and source of each film, tape, or slide.

4. *Evaluation.* Just before the end of the class, the instructor will (or will ask you to) hand out evaluation forms to all participants and ask them to fill them out immediately. As they leave the class, you will collect the completed form from each one.

5. *Skill assessment survey.* Approximately two weeks after the class, you will conduct a brief telephone interview with the participants. During the inter-

(continued on next page)

Figure 6 (Continued)

view you will ask them to rate the class on a number of quality indicators and to evaluate their own class experience. They will also be asked to estimate how much they learned and to assess their first-aid skills before and after the class.

Training

During today's meeting, you will receive information on and practice the study's tasks. If you have any questions, please be sure to raise them during the meeting. The district schedulers will act as supervisors and will be available to give you any assistance you need. After the meeting, please review the instructions before your first assignment.

Assignments

Each staff member will be trained in all of the tasks and may be assigned to any of the classes in his or her district. At the end of the training session, you will receive your assignments for the first week. Later assignments will be mailed to you. If for any reason you cannot accept an assignment, be sure to notify the scheduler for your district as soon as possible. Schedulers are:

District				
District 1	South Newburg County, outside of Alton	Ed Peek	224-3166
2	Alton City	Agnes Wilson	483-9054
3	North Newburg (North of Coal Creek)	Sue Rustone	347-6297
4	Algona (East Algona, Firville, Santon)	Bill Johnson	362-4683
5	Bellevue and South Hampton	Jill Conrad	363-9768
6	Western County North of State Road 56	Nicole Brill	432-0670
7	Western County between I-90 and SR-56	Steve Gillow	833-4645

Supervision

The scheduler for your district will act as your supervisor. He or she will arrange with you for a convenient meeting time to review your work and will set up a schedule for contacting you as the study progresses. If at any time you need assistance, call your supervisor or the project office in Algona, 362-0400 (collect).

Time Schedules

The study will start immediately and continue throughout the month.

Office Procedures

You will sign your employment papers at the meeting and will be given your employee ID number at that time. Be sure that this number appears with your name on all the hourly reports and expense vouchers you submit. They cannot be processed for payment without it. You must also complete a tax option authorization at this time. Filling out these papers will be explained and demonstrated in the meeting.

Pay rates for this study are $4.00 per hour for work done on weekdays between 9 a.m. and 5 p.m. Work during classes which meet in the evenings and on weekends will be paid at the rate of $4.25 per hour. Travel to classes will be reimbursed at $.16 per mile. Meals will not be reimbursed.

Figure 6 (Continued)

Hourly reports (time worked) and travel vouchers (mileage) must be submitted every Tuesday for all work done through the previous Sunday. Paychecks will be distributed on the 1st and 15th of the month, for work done through the 15th of the preceding month and the 1st of the current month, respectively.

Trainees should receive a copy of the material before or at the beginning of the meeting. They should also have a copy of the agenda, as an outline of the training they will have.

Figure 7. Sample of Training Agenda

Western County Fire District 103
First-Aid Course Evaluation
Training Meeting Agenda—November 6, 1978

8:30 a.m.	Welcome by Chief Haskins
9:00	Introduction of staff and guests
9:15	Background of the research project—Carl Swensen, Director
10:00	Review of scheduling and work assignments
	Completion of employment papers
10:20	Break (coffee available in lounge)
10:30	Description and instruction on tasks
	1. Applicants and attendees tally—Wilson
	2. Class topics recording—Johnson
	3. Audiovisual materials recording—Brill
	4. Evaluation—Peek
12:00	Lunch
1:00 p.m.	Review of tasks 1-4
1:30	5. Skill assessment survey—Rustone and Gillow
3:00	Break (coffee available in lounge)
3:15	Practice on skill assessment survey
4:00	Practice on topics recording
4:20	Practice on audiovisual recording
4:45	Review of assignments
	Final remarks

Amplified by the trainer's notes, the agenda as written for the research team would appear:

8:30 a.m.   Welcome by Chief Haskins (He will describe typical first-aid class. He

97

9:00

9:15

10:00

10:30

speaks very loudly, turn down mike)

Introduction of staff and guests (Obtain biographical data for introductions, check titles)

Background of the research project (Show timeline for project—call on Jan to discuss national research)

Review of scheduling and work assignments (Calendar, maps marked to indicate locations and dates; information on schedule)

Completion of employment papers (Sample forms, instructions. Hand out blank forms, collect, check for completeness, provide insurance brochure)

Description and instruction on tasks

1. Applicants and attendees tally (Show, demonstrate use of tally sheets; provide information on how to explain activities to attendees)

2. Class topics recording (Show, demonstrate use of record sheet; demonstrate and practice use of stop watch; present glossary of terms)

3. Audiovisual materials recording (Show, demonstrate record forms; identify types of media, provide information on locating names of producers, distributers, etc.)

4. Evaluation (Show, demonstrate

		forms; instruct on how to present evaluation if class instructor does not)
1:30 p.m.	5.	Skill assessment survey (Instruction on questionnaire items, methods of contacting participants)
3:15		Practice on skill assessment survey (Practice on conducting interview, role playing)
4:00		Practice on topics recording (Examples of segments of class presentations; quiz on timing and topics cited)
4:20		Practice on audiovisual recording (Examples of media presentations; quiz on timing and records)
4:45		Review of assignments (Distribution of assignments, explanation of schedules, answer questions)

The complete script for the various parts of the training does not have to be written, but a clear scenario of events should at least be prepared. The segment of the training on Task 2, for example, might run according to this plan:

2. *Class topics recording*
    Trainer (to trainees): You will record the topics covered in the class on the light-blue class record sheets (show blown-up copy on wall chart; pass out copies).
    You will notice that there is a space at the top left (point out) for the date, time, and location of the class. Fill this out before the class starts. At the top right, there is space for your name and ID number (point out).

Field Research

Below the heading, there are numbered lines for the topics (point out).

Every subject that the class covers is a topic. Topics include general introductory remarks about first aid; specific instruction about injuries, symptoms, and treatment; instructions and demonstrations of treatment; question or discussion periods; and quizzes. For example, these would be topics:

> Showing the location of blood vessels on a chart or model
>
> Describing the appearance of someone in shock
>
> Demonstrating cardiopulmonary resuscitation techniques
>
> Students practicing techniques on each other
>
> Tests on knowledge
>
> Questions by students about what is taught

Examples of class activities which are *not* topics would be:

> Signing up for tours or special exhibits on first aid
>
> Conversations about personal or social matters
>
> Discussion of plans for further training or advanced classes

(Show filmstrip on types of class activity; quiz trainees on identification of eligible topics.)

You will record the topics by writing a brief description of one topic on each line (give examples of descriptive phrases for various topics).

In the next box, b, after the description, circle the word *Instructor, Student,* or *Other* to show who introduced the topic; that is, who first mentioned it (point out). If it was an *Other*, such as a guest, note this on the line. (Make sure the trainees understand these concepts. Review as necessary.)

Now, you'll notice that the next box, c, asks for the time the class spent on the topic. To measure the time, you'll use a stop watch (hand out stop watches, show filmstrip on operation, practice use of stop watch on timed incidents).

At a later point, the trainer would show filmed excerpts of classes and have the trainees fill out their records under supervision. Preparation of the training in such detail is well worth the trouble if it creates a group of staff members able to work in the field with minimal uncertainty. Preparation for each of the segments of the meeting would probably call for at least an implicit operations schedule, to make sure that the forms to be explained are available, that the maps displayed are accurately marked, and that the stop watches distributed work as they should.

Where training takes place is also important. The meeting room must be convenient and suitable for the training activities. Its acoustics must be good, so that the occupants can hear what is said; it must be well lighted; and it must contain appropriate wall space for illustrations. As in all other fieldwork, selecting and setting up your training location calls for advance planning. You must be sure that the location is identified so that people can find it and that the equipment you need is ready. Staff members, like subjects, should find that work on your project is efficient and organized. Your preliminary walk-through will allow you to identify the doorways that must be marked and to note which switch lowers the screen and which turns on the ventilator. It will also enable you to tell trainees that the vending machine is down the hall to the right but that the telephone is in the lower lobby and requires coins.

In many instances, the researchers' principal contact with the field staff occurs during training. The staff may be known to you only as voices over the telephone before and as the producers of data afterward. It is at the training that you can gain some indication of how knowledgeable and quick to learn the trainees are and whether they work diligently. Your most important role during training may be observation—of how well you have prepared the materials to be presented and of how well they are received. If you set up the meeting and prepare the presentation carefully, you will be free to work actively with the trainees and to make sure that they learn what they must know.

Subcontracting

There is one way to avoid the difficulties of recruiting, training, and supervising a field staff: You can buy any or all of these services from an organization that produces and sells them. Such organizations call themselves research services, consulting groups, survey teams, think tanks, planning companies, or similar titles, and they are eager to contract with the researcher for the conduct of field projects. The costs and benefits of such a transaction are easily calculated. At best, you may procure the specialized skills of a highly qualified professional and spare yourself the difficulties of creating, from the beginning, the research structures you will use. At worst, you will place your work in the hands of some mercenary outsiders who have little regard for your needs and standards. In reality, subcontracting is usually neither best nor worst. What you buy, in these circumstances, is a small temporary share in an ongoing fieldwork enterprise, over which you have little influence. The cost is paid both in money and in loss of control over parts of the project. Depending on the circumstances, it may be either a bargain or a serious error.

The original operations plan and cost estimates will have provided you with accurate information on how much, in effort and money, the field activities will cost. These estimates will contain quality specifications and time schedules and should include a realistic appraisal of the value of your time. Armed with this information, you are in a position to evaluate the comparative worth of any services that are offered. In research, as in any other area, quality costs either time or money. If you wish to conserve your own efforts, others must be paid to expend theirs. The primary concern should be not with the cost of the product but with its worth to you. If you choose to hire others to carry out the project, stipulate the extent of your own involvement. A conscientious and ethical research service will not only welcome but will require your participation. Remember, however, that lessening your involvement in any aspect of your work carries a cost in terms of your own control over it. You may gain, rather than lose, by relinquishing responsibility, but it should not be given up casually.

Six

Cost Estimates, Budgeting, and Money Management

❖◆❖◆❖◆❖◆❖◆❖◆❖◆❖◆❖◆❖◆❖◆❖◆❖◆❖◆❖◆❖◆❖◆❖

Like all other human activities, field research must be paid for. Even a project that requires only your own efforts carries hidden opportunity costs, in terms of the value of what else you might be doing instead of the research. Time, materials, and services, for the most part, are translated into money. You may plan to finance the work by yourself, or you may have access to funds provided by some granting agency or sponsoring organization. No matter what the source of the money, you must be able to predict how much will be needed, control the rate at which it is spent, and account

105

for it afterward. The information you need to manage this aspect of the research arises out of the operations schedule and the decisions you have made about the people and materials necessary to conduct the work. You will begin by estimating the costs of the materials, services, and efforts that your research requires.

Sufficient money to meet your estimates should be on hand or allocated to your project before the study begins. Doing fieldwork commits you to agreements with people and institutions in the real world. It is difficult to explain to a store owner whose premises you have requisitioned for a demonstration or a librarian who has made over space for your data storage that the money has run out and your project has been canceled. Any redesign or changes that result from scaling down your project should be made before the work starts; adding to the study once it is in the field is inefficient, but attempting to cut it back can be disastrous. You should be prepared to explain and defend your estimates, and modify them if necessary. Recognize the right and the obligation to demand adequate resources for the work to be done. It is typical of researchers, eager to investigate a fascinating problem, to be optimistic about funding. If the project is irresistible to you, you may feel that it is equally enticing to the people who control the money, so that, once the work has started, the funds will magically appear to complete it. Sometimes this happens; more often it does not. Your estimates should be carefully calculated and reasonable, but they should also be considered as minimal requirements. If the minimum is not available, you would be best advised to plan something else.

Insisting on adequate resources does not sanction extravagance. Researchers, like everyone else, must concern themselves with economy. However, economy refers to the wise use of resources, not simply to minimizing expenditures. The cheapest solution is frequently not the most economical one. In many instances, money is the cheapest thing you have. Most people act upon this concept, by their willingness to exchange money for other things they want, even though they may not recognize the principle on which they are acting. Saving money is desirable when it does not interfere with the activities for which the money is being spent; sometimes, however, money must be spent freely if a field research project is to be protected. At such times, it is well to remember that the primary aim is to accomplish the tasks. Justifying their costs should be done when the project budget is established, and after the tasks are completed. Few projects, and even fewer researchers, are granted unlimited resources. The cost estimates you make and the financial records you maintain are essential in documenting and accounting for what you have done.

Cost Estimates

As soon as you have listed all the tasks to be accomplished and all the resources that will be needed, you can estimate how much your field project will cost. Supplies, materials, transportation, and services usually have fixed costs. It is not difficult to calculate the amount that must be spent on pencils at $1.29 for a box of twenty or for the rent of a projector at so much per day. The costs of people's efforts are more complicated to calculate but still can be estimated with some degree of precision. How much to allow for unexpected problems depends on the characteristics of the research tasks, the ease with which the site can be reached, and the resources of the participants.

Your operations schedule will provide a list of all of the supplies and materials to be used and the time when they are needed. From this list, you can develop cost estimates by assigning a money value to each element. Remember that services, as well as supplies, cost money and that materials to be reused at different times may need to be repaired or replenished. Moreover, materials not in constant use will have to be stored and transported to and from their place of use. Your estimates must allow for all these costs.

107

Field Research

For example, a graduate student in sociology decided to write her master's thesis on the gender-linked career aspirations of fourth-grade public school students. To test her hypothesis—that there is a relationship between the child's sex, the mother's occupation, and the child's career aspiration—she would have to administer a questionnaire to the children in their classrooms. She received permission to conduct the survey from the local school system, which was planning to implement a career preparation program in the elementary grades and thus anticipated benefits from the study. The sociology department approved the project and authorized the student to receive a $50 research grant to fund the work. In addition, the department agreed to pay for photocopying the questionnaires and the consent forms that the children would be required to take home for their parents' signatures; only those children who received parental permission would be included in the study. The plans called for the researcher to visit the classrooms, explain the study to the pupils, show slides of people doing various kinds of work, distribute the questionnaire, and pick it up after the children had completed it. The regular classroom teacher, after introducing the researcher, would leave the class and would wait in the lounge or library until the survey was done. A meeting with all the teachers was scheduled for the week prior to the study, to familiarize them with the project.

The actual costs of the project could be estimated from the operations schedule, as shown in Figure 8. The materials needed were consent letters for parents, slides, questionnaires, pencils, envelopes for storing separate class data, and explanatory memos for the classroom teachers. The sociology department would duplicate the questionnaires, letters, and memos. Telephone calls to several stores located a source of pencils at 7 cents each, in quantities of one hundred or more. Allowing thirty at a time for each class, and for some of the pencils to be lost or broken, she purchased one hundred. Large envelopes for storing the completed questionnaires cost 40 cents each, or $12 for thirty classes. The slide projector could be borrowed in each

Figure 8. Operations Schedule for Children's Career Aspirations Study

Task	Subtasks	Location	Materials	Time	Staff
Familiarize teachers with study	(a) Write memo	Office		October 4	Researcher
	(b) Meet with teachers	Highland School Administration Building, Room 15	Memos, questionnaires, consent forms, introductory letter from chairman of department, research design statement, projector, slides	October 10, 1:30 (teachers' in-service workshop)	Researcher
	(c) Show slides, demonstrate questionnaire				
Get parental consent	(a) Send letters to parents	School classrooms	Letters, consent forms, tally sheets	Week of October 14	Classroom teachers
	(b) Follow-up (phone)	University	List of phone numbers	Week of October 21	Researcher
Conduct survey	(a) Schedule visits	University	List of classrooms, school time schedules	October 28-November 9	Researcher, school secretary
	(b) Show slides	Classrooms	Slides, projector (check out of school supply rooms)		Researcher
	(c) Hand out, pick up questionnaires		Questionnaires, envelopes, pencils		

school, but duplicating the set of twelve slides cost $18. The cost to the researcher thus was estimated at $37. What did not enter into this calculation were several other elements. The researcher drove to each of the schools at which the survey was conducted. While she did not think of the gas she used and the depreciation on her car as project expenditures, these were actual costs, as were the lunches she bought while she was in the field and the coffee cakes she supplied for the teachers' lounges while the classroom teachers were waiting there. The costs for transportation and food were buried in the researcher's household budget, but they were nevertheless charges that should have been assigned to the research project.

Since the researcher expected to work alone, assisted only by the classroom teachers in obtaining the parental consent form, she did not concern herself with calculating the human costs of the work. In this instance, she expected to contribute her own time and trusted that the teachers would be equally willing to volunteer theirs. Being inexperienced, both with field research and with children, she seriously underestimated the amount of effort required. The teachers were interested in the study and accepted the decision of the school district to participate in the research, but they considered it secondary to their regular classroom activities. Thus, although the teachers did remember to give the children consent forms to take home, they paid little attention to which ones were returned. In a few cases, when parents asked the teachers about the study, they received inadequate or misleading information. Quite naturally, many parents failed to sign and send back the forms. On October 21, when the researcher checked with the schools on the receipt of the consent forms, she was astonished by the number of parents who would have to be called for permission. She had not allowed sufficient time in her schedule for this task and therefore had to recruit someone to help her. Another graduate student, the mother of several children, agreed to help, and the two succeeded in contacting most of the parents. Between phone calls, the older woman pointed out some of the difficulties of dealing with large numbers of children and advised that a second person go along to the schools. By this time, the researcher had also discovered that the school's traditional Halloween celebrations would take up several school days during the first week of the survey. An additional person would enable the surveys to be conducted in more than one classroom at a time and thus speed the work. The researcher asked the older student to participate in these activities and offered to pay for the other woman's time. A duplicate set of slides was purchased for the older woman's use.

The project was completed on time, but several of the researcher's problems lasted longer. When she applied to her department for payment of her expenses under the grant, the largest of her claims was disallowed. She had not cleared employment of an assistant with the department in advance, and the woman could not be paid out of grant funds. The clerk pointed out, however, that mileage charges could be listed for travel to the research site. The coffee cakes, considered as rewards to subjects, were also allowed, although coffee and lunches which the researcher bought for herself and her assistant did not qualify. The researcher finally offered to pay her assistant out of her own pocket. The woman refused the money but suggested that the researcher could compensate her by babysitting with her children while she studied for exams. The researcher, spending her afternoons with the children and cramming her own studying into the evenings, was made forcibly aware of the equivalence of time and money.

In this case, what the mother got was not measured in dollars. Most field research personnel, however, expect to be paid for their efforts. How much they are paid depends on who they are and what they do. If you are to do all or most of the work by yourself, it is easy to figure out what it will cost. You know how much you earn, or what you need to live on, and can project this sum forward over the length of the project. The researcher working alone, or sharing tasks with a limited number of coworkers, will perform at different levels of skill, as the project demands. Individuals and members of small teams will expect to move boxes of supplies, staple booklets, train interviewers, make coffee, or lead discussion groups with little regard for job titles. As the size of the group increases, however, differentiation occurs. Staff members with special qualifications can be selected to operate in their area of greatest skill, and the research manager can begin to assign tasks with some concern for cost-effectiveness. Fieldwork being what it is, the highest-paid staff members will sometimes run errands, or the most junior statistician will suddenly have to assume responsibility for a major operation; but for the most part larger teams can utilize their members more economically.

When field research requires the coordinated efforts of many people, cost estimates must be based on a realistic projection of the person/hours needed. Assigning a value, in money or some other reward, to each person/hour enables you to estimate the costs of that element of the work. Remember that the cost you assign is attached to the task, not to the person. Thus, if a particular part of the work can be done by a number of people, each paid at a different rate per hour, it is to your advantage to assign that task to the lowest-paid qualified person and estimate its cost as a function of the low rate. It is inefficient to pay more than is necessary. Where the field project consists of many different types of work, and each requires many hours of effort, you can establish a work force that fills the slots with maximum economy.

Field research usually falls somewhere between the efforts of a solitary researcher and the massive enterprise that benefits from cost analysis. When the graduate student previously referred to decided to hire an assistant, she crossed the line from individual researcher to manager of a research team. Along with the advantages she gained from her assistant's efforts, she took on the responsibility for training, supervising, and paying for the assistant's work. Some portion of her own time was necessarily spent on these activities. Supervisory time is not productive and must be subtracted from the total. The cost of supervision and management becomes part of the sum when personnel needs are established.

If you have planned your project carefully, the costs of conducting the study are predictable, and the estimates should be close to the actual expenditures. You can expect, however, that some things you have not planned will occur. The cost estimates should include some amount to cover situations that cannot be predicted. It is difficult to make accurate estimates about what will go wrong. If your project is like work that has been done before, under similar circumstances, and if the previous researchers can remember and are willing to warn you about the pitfalls, you can be prepared for at least some of the problems. But successful outcomes tend to wash out memories of what went wrong; the researcher who fought through immense inconveniences and errors to complete the work may recall only, a few years later, that "I had some staff trouble" or "It was hard to get cooperation after they found out we were moving the station."

Money to assist you in coping with unexpected situations should be available, although it does not have to be on hand. It can take the form of a bank deposit or credit card, to be drawn on only if necessary, or it can be the willingness of some member of your team to assume responsibility for paying bills until additional funds arrive. These additional emergency funds or credit should be considered as part of the estimated costs. If they are not used, they can be returned. But without them your project may fail.

Budgeting and Money Management

Distribution of resources over the time period and requirements of the study is the function of the budget. The plan and the estimates of needs and costs specify how much will be spent on each element. A budget is the operational statement of these specifications, telling you, for instance, that no more than one sixth of the total supply allocation should be spent each month for the six months of the project, or that investment in a camera, paid for at the beginning of the fieldwork, can be charged off proportionately against each of twelve conferences. The budget can also serve as an accounting tool, notifying you of how much has been spent and how much remains. It thus provides guidance on the rate of expenditure and allows you to monitor progress of the work against its cost.

The degree of control which the researcher has over the budget varies with the parent organization and the source of funding. Individuals working with their own money, or responsible only for a final accounting of some lump sum payment, can modify their financial procedures, shift money from one category of expenditure to another, or pay bills in whatever form or at whatever time seems convenient. These researchers are still subject to some need for reporting where their money went, even if only to themselves and their spouses, but they may be able to postpone or simplify the reckoning almost at will. In contrast, students or employees of large institutions may have almost no control over how money is managed on a day-to-day basis. Once the budget for a project is set, most of it operates automatically through the institution's mechanisms. There are, of course, wide variations in how such mechanisms work in practice. Thus, a graduate student conducting dissertation research at a field installation may receive a stipend on a regular basis from the university and, in turn, submit expense vouchers for accounting at a later date. Under other circumstances, the student may receive a research grant in cash, to be accounted for only at the end of the project. An intermediate situation might be one in which a salaried staff member working in the field receives monthly paychecks but can apply for a cash advance to cover her out-of-pocket expenses before settlement at the end of the study.

Keeping track of the project's money is a necessary task and must be assigned to a responsible person, who is kept apprised of all expenditures. The convenience of casual accounting during a project is paid for afterward. The researcher who receives a telephone call from a federal auditor inquiring about an $11 petty cash voucher misplaced four years earlier learns the lesson, as does a staff member who is called on to account for the dimes and quarters given to children who helped retrieve floats spilled off the dock where the oceanographic vessel tied up. In both cases, neglect of what had appeared to be unimportant and unnecessary paperwork caused time-consuming searches through inadequate records long after the researchers had moved on to other projects.

The form in which money appears also affects how it can be used in fieldwork. A person who works within an organization can conduct research for years without ever dealing directly with money. Researchers and their parent institutions generate and exchange purchase orders, requisitions, pay vouchers, cost transfer memos, credit, budget allocations, and encumbrances. Rarely do they handle cash. The field, however, is part of the money economy. The pieces of paper that are the medium of exchange in the organization are meaningless outside its system. They must be translated into currency, or into a form such as a bill or a check that is recognized as valuable, and can be absorbed into the economic system in which ordinary transactions are made. Reconciling these divergent systems can become an important research task.

Despite your efforts to provide field workers with everything they require, there will be many occasions when money has to be spent. A staff member may be delayed and need 15 cents to telephone his apologies, a subject may be won to cooperation only over numerous cups of coffee, or the discovery of missing supplies may mean substantial outlays of cash at a drugstore or supermarket. Senior researchers may have adequate money in hand, but this is not likely to be true for everyone. Particularly when staff members are recruited in the field, from among the subject population, providing gas to drive to a meeting or replacing a defective film cassette on the experimental site may prove a real hardship. An example:

A study of social affiliation among minority teenagers

used interviewers from the same community to collect data during various types of social activities. After an evening basketball game between two of the experimental groups, an older woman interviewer stayed behind to complete her work with the last team members. She then found herself, at 10:00 p.m., alone in the community center of a disreputable neighborhood. She was properly reluctant to travel home by herself and persuaded the caretaker to let her use the office telephone before he locked up the building. She called her supervisor to ask for help.

The supervisor, at home miles away in the suburbs, suggested "Call a cab. The project will pay for it." The interviewer resisted the notion, at first politely, and then with increasing discomfort apparent in her voice. It took a few minutes to identify the source of the interviewer's embarrassment, but finally the supervisor realized that the interviewer had no money to pay the cab fare, even though she would be reimbursed at the end of the month. It took some time before the supervisor could call the cab company, arrange to have the fare put on his bank charge card, and convince the custodian that he should allow the interviewer to wait safely inside the center until the taxi came, but that was still easier than driving into the city to provide her escort home. Negotiating repayment through his organization's travel expenditure voucher procedures was a task the supervisor dealt with at a later time.

It is hard for properly brought-up people to ask questions about other people's resources. But a supervisor sometimes has to ask "Do you need money to buy gas?" or "Shall I advance you enough to get your briefcase fixed?" or "Have you change for the phone?" Getting such information without appearing patronizing or condescending requires tact. It can be even more difficult when the money is to be used for personal expenses rather than strictly research-connected costs. Supplying cash or a credit card to buy research supplies or transportation does not call for much excuse. Where the researcher feels that a field worker needs to have his hair cut or his shoes repaired before he represents the organization, offering to pay for such expenses can be humiliating to the staff member and embarrassing to the researcher. A good researcher will be able to relate such requests to the needs of the study and therefore spare both parties discomfort.

Authorizing the use of cash, and accounting for it afterward, may be a complicated process. Most organizations have regulations that restrict the use of cash and make it necessary for workers to justify spending and collecting it. From the viewpoint of the organization, this is a sensible arrangement, since it provides control over expenditures. In the field, it can be extremely inconvenient. You may want to apply for some sort of cash advance or make sure that one of your field staff routinely carries enough money to pay for unexpected expenses. Learn what your organization's rules are and how to follow them most efficiently. Do special forms have to be filled out and submitted? Find out who must sign them, and have a supply ready to use. How quickly can requests for money be filled? Look for ways to speed the process. There are usually emergency procedures which can be invoked, if you know them. What kind of accounting is required? Make sure that your staff members know what kind of records to keep and how to document these expenditures.

It is unreasonable to ask that individuals support the activities of the organizations they work for, even on a temporary basis, but this occurs frequently under field conditions. Staff members involved in field operations are usually sufficiently committed to their projects to use their own money for essential expenses, under emergency conditions, but you cannot demand that they do. Part of your responsibility is to minimize the need for such sacrifices and to make sure that they are promptly repaid. Over the long run, if you have planned your work properly, expenses and reimbursements usually balance. In the short term, the need for immediate expenditures can seriously threaten your work. Preparing for such problems is essential.

Faced with circumstances that demand more money than

you have, what should you do? Your choices are limited. You can attempt to obtain more money, spend less, or seek a compromise between these two alternatives. The simplest step, although not necessarily the easiest, is to obtain more. If you are funding the study by yourself, you must decide how much it is worth to you in comparison with other needs. The value of the study depends on the use you intend to make of its products. Dissertation or thesis research is of great importance; the student who reaches this stage in graduate school has already invested years of effort in his or her education. Cutting short or canceling a field project may mean losing this investment. The student who must make this choice will probably borrow money, moonlight, impress the unpaid labor of friends and relatives, and do work for which others would expect to be paid. When the value of the study is lower, of course, the researcher will be more likely to sacrifice it. Most investigators are familiar with studies that are left incomplete or scaled down to fit restricted budgets.

Research sponsored by an organization or agency may be salvaged. Asking for more money to do work which has run over budget may be embarrassing, but it is often successful. The granting agency, too, has an investment to protect. You may be asked to resubmit the proposal or recalculate the budget, but the funds will usually be granted. Whether your next proposal to that source is accepted is another matter.

Scaling down or cutting short your project to fit the budget entails making other decisions. A design modification that permits shrinking some fixed portion of each element will allow you to reduce the project proportionately across all activities. For example, if a testing program threatens to run over budget, you can drop a certain number of subjects from each group to be tested; similarly, you can scale down a longitudinal program by stretching the intervals between follow-up visits, thus requiring fewer trips over the scheduled time. Unfortunately, the discovery that you have run out of money often occurs suddenly, when it is too late to modify your design. Under these circumstances, it may be necessary to seek other sources of funding or to drop some portion of your study. If you must eliminate one or more elements, make sure that they are self-contained units and that the other parts of the study will not be affected. An example:

A staff member of the board of education proposed a study of the feasibility of developing a program in coaching high school competitive athletics for women. The design contained four elements: an analysis of the existing pattern of coaching assignments among teachers, a survey of school administrators' opinions on the desirability of implementing sex-specific criteria for selection of coaches, a survey of teachers' interest in participating in such a program, and an evaluation of sex bias in existing literature on coaching. A workshop for teachers was to be included in the teacher interest survey, and the administrators were to be interviewed in person at their schools. The results were to be reported to universities and teacher training institutions. The staff member's calculations of the resources required and the cost estimates she developed for the work were based on the number of hours of activity at various salary levels, plus the costs of the materials and services to be purchased. The budget, as presented for approval, is shown in Figure 9. The policies of the board of education required that employee benefits be charged against the particular work unit, so that an item of 16 percent was added to the personnel costs for each element of the study.

Figure 9. Budget for Feasibility Study

Element 1. Analysis of Existing Teacher Assignment Patterns
    A. Design of data collection procedures and instruments

Principal investigator (PI)	32 hours at	$9.00	
Clerical	20	5.00	$ 388.00

    B. Correspondence with school officials, state offices, and teachers

PI	20	9.00	
Secretary	30	5.50	345.00

(continued on next page)

119

Figure 9 (Continued)

C. Data collection			
Clerical	80	4.00	
Supervisory	20	6.00	440.00
D. Data entry (keypunching)	60	5.50	330.00
E. Programming	4	11.00	44.00
F. Analysis and report			
PI	40	9.00	
Statistician	16	7.50	
Clerical (graphing)	16	5.00	560.00
TOTAL WAGES AND SALARIES			$ 2,107.00
Benefits at 16%			337.00
TOTAL PERSONNEL COSTS			$ 2,444.00
Purchase of data tape			140.00
Computer time			155.00
Telephone and postage			75.00
Supplies and materials			185.00
Travel to state capital (2 trips) mileage 400 at $.16			
meals 20.00			84.00
TOTAL STUDY ELEMENT COSTS			$ 3,083.00

Element 2. Survey of School Administrators' Opinion			
A. Design of data collection procedures and instruments			
PI	24 hours at	9.00	
Secretary	40	5.00	$ 416.00
B. Data collection			
Telephone interviews	400	4.50	
Supervisory	10	7.00	
Clerical (logging, records)	30	4.50	2,005.00
C. Data reduction			
Editing and verifying	30	4.75	
Data entry	4	5.50	164.50
D. Programming	2	11.00	22.00
E. Analysis and report			
PI	24	9.00	
Clerical (graphing)	20	5.00	316.00
TOTAL WAGES AND SALARIES			$ 2,923.50
Benefits at 16%			468.00
TOTAL PERSONNEL COSTS			$ 3,391.50
Travel (6,000 miles at $.16)			960.00
Computer time			65.00
Telephone			30.00
Supplies			50.00
Printing			190.00
Postage			40.00
TOTAL STUDY ELEMENT COSTS			$ 4,726.50

Figure 9 (Continued)

Element 3. Survey of Interest Among Teachers
A. Design of procedures and instruments

PI	20 hours at	9.00	
Clerical	8	4.50	$ 216.00

B. Data collection

Addressing, stuffing, and mailing	40	4.00	
Supervisory	8	7.00	
Clerical	40	4.00	376.00

C. Workshops

PI	20	9.00	
Research assistants (2)	40	6.00	420.00

D. Data reduction

Editing and verifying	500	3.50	
Data entry	80	5.50	2,190.00

E. Programming

	6	11.00	66.00

F. Analysis and report

PI	48	9.00	
Secretary	30	5.00	582.00
TOTAL WAGES AND SALARIES			$ 3,850.00
Benefits at 16%			616.00
TOTAL PERSONNEL COSTS			$ 4,466.00
Computer			150.00
Supplies (12 boxes of envelopes at $10.50, misc.)			200.00
Printing			325.00
Postage (1st mailing, 2 follow-up, return)			800.00
Conference fees, room rental, program ad, posters (workshops)			425.00
TOTAL STUDY ELEMENT COSTS			$ 6,366.00

Element 4. Literature Evaluation
A. Design

PI	12 hours at	9.00	
Secretary	8	5.50	$ 152.00

B. Data collection

Research assistant (RA)	480	6.00	
Clerical	12	4.00	2,928.00

C. Analysis and report

PI	24	9.00	
RA	24	6.00	
Secretary	24	5.50	492.00
TOTAL WAGES AND SALARIES			$ 3,572.00
Benefits at 16%			572.00
TOTAL PERSONNEL COSTS			$ 4,144.00

(continued on next page)

121

Figure 9 (Continued)

Purchase and/or rent of materials	900.00
TOTAL STUDY ELEMENT COSTS	$ 5,044.00
TOTAL COST ESTIMATE	$19,219.50

After considering the proposal, the board's research committee informed the investigator that her study was approved in principle but that there was little money available. They suggested that she rewrite and resubmit her plan, scaled down, for a special grant program. These grants, however, were limited to a total under $10,000. The researcher reviewed her proposal with a number of other people in her field and identified the following economies. The specific modifications, and the amounts saved in each, are shown below.

1. The data base for the analysis of teacher assignment patterns was permanently available at the state office of public instruction. Since these records could be consulted at a later time, this element of the study was postponed, at a saving of $3,083 on the original proposal.

2. One of the researcher's colleagues was knowledgeable about Affirmative Action issues and was engaged in negotiations with several teacher groups who were challenging school systems. This colleague pointed out that asking school administrators how they felt about sex-specific selection criteria was irrelevant, since the question would be decided in the courts. This element was therefore dropped, at a saving of $4,726.50.

3. The survey of teachers' interest was reexamined for possible scaling down. The teachers' sample had been planned to include 25 percent of all teachers in the state's high schools, a group of approximately 8,500. Suspecting that the sample was needlessly large, the researcher consulted a sampling statistician, who assured her that a 10 percent sample would be sufficient. The sample list was pruned accordingly. The survey of interest had originally been planned to coincide with a meeting of the state teachers' association and to include workshops at the

meeting for the respondents. The researcher was unable to demonstrate that the workshops would produce data not obtainable elsewhere; the workshops were accordingly eliminated, and references to them dropped from the questionnaires and meeting notices. Those costs which were directly attributable to specific quantities of effort or products could be reduced proportionately. Thus, the number of hours of data reduction and collection was trimmed by approximately 50 percent. Supervisory costs, however, continued at the same figure, as did the estimates for design, analysis, and reporting. It took as long to write the report on 850 cases as on 2,200. Postage and supplies were reduced by the exact factor of sample size, and the conference expenses, of course, no longer were entered. The savings by this modification were estimated as $2,909.

4. The evaluation of sex bias in the literature was considered too important to the study to be reduced, although its cost in staff time at a professional level was high. After consulting with faculty members at the local university, the researcher was able to arrange with an instructor in English for a cooperative investigation. A graduate class in the Department of English agreed to study the materials as a term project in bias in communication and to prepare the report for delivery to the board. The total costs to the board for this element thus became only the sum for purchase of materials, and a few hours of the principal investigator's time in organizing joint effort. The research was redesigned to meet the budget available for it. As modified, the total estimate for the study came to approximately $8,700, an amount acceptable to the granting agency.

There is a point, however, beyond which a study cannot be starved. If reasonable efforts to adapt your proposal to available resources are not successful in producing a coherent and manageable design, do something else.

Seven

---◆---

Materials,
Supplies,
and Suppliers

◆◆◆◆◆◆◆◆◆◆◆◆◆◆◆◆◆◆◆◆◆◆◆◆◆◆◆◆◆◆◆◆◆◆◆◆◆◆

Research also requires things—
to be worked on by subjects, tallied or filled in by researchers,
or used to process and document results. Every item that will be
used in the study must be procured and brought to the research
site, in adequate quantity, and at the proper time. Borrowing
supplies and equipment, or using services of the site, presents an
unattractive view of your competence. The subject population
is usually willing to lend pencils or a stapler, and to photocopy
the materials you failed to count accurately. But these same
subjects may suspect that you are disorganized or unprepared to

do your work, and that suspicion is bound to affect their participation. You should plan to be, to as great an extent as possible, independent of the research site's resources. The environmentalists' rule, to pack in and take out everything that is used, is a good one to follow, and for the same reason. It makes the least impact on the surroundings and thus minimizes the contamination of your research findings. Many of the items required will be the ordinary supplies used to carry on any business: typewriters, paper clips, note pads, and similar familiar tools. Typically, the researcher *has* these things; they are available at or near his desk or in a handy supply cupboard. Someone else orders them and makes sure that there are pencils in the pencil box and enough paper stacked up beside the mimeograph machine for routine operations. In the field, you are that person, responsible for supplying the tools you and your staff will use.

Determining Needs

How can you determine what supplies you will need? Again, "walking through" your procedures can be very helpful. Note what materials are used for every separate action you perform. These items should be recorded in the most precise detail. Does your plan require that workers will be interviewed as they leave the plant? Will you use a pencil or a pen? What will their answers be written on? How will you provide a writing surface? Where will you keep the blank questionnaires, and how will you separate them from those already completed? If you will be outdoors, can you protect yourself and the respondents from the weather? What about keeping your materials dry? Answering these questions will give you the information you will need to prepare a list of materials for the study. An important part of this process is specification: making explicit the criteria by which you can determine whether an object or event meets your requirements. Specifying such characteristics is necessary both for materials you procure and for those which are found in the research setting. You must define things before you can count or measure them. An example:

A study of exposure to election appeals and voting behavior required that a count of election signs and posters in a particular neighborhood be made. The distance between these signs and a selected sample of housing units would be measured and a count kept of the number of cars with candidate or election issue bumper stickers which parked within the study area or passed the nearest major street intersections during the times when neighborhood residents were outdoors. On the evening before the election, the subjects and a matched control sample of residents would be interviewed by telephone, to obtain information about intention to vote. During the hours when the polls were open on election day, a tally would be kept of which sample and control group members actually voted. The operations plan specified the tasks as follows:

TASK	SUBTASKS
1. Count signs and posters	a. Define various types of signs b. Establish criteria for identification c. Count
2. Measure distances	a. Define (specify) measuring points b. Select standard of measure c. Measure distances
3. Count cars with stickers in study area	a. Define (specify) political stickers b. Establish boundaries of study area c. Specify street intersections d. Determine appropriate time periods e. Count cars

Notice that the first subtask of the first task required that the researchers define what they meant by a sign or poster. Would a chalked slogan on a brick wall qualify? If Candidate Bloggs campaigned on a platform of conservation and ecology, would a poster that said "Protect Whales" count as an election advertisement? What about defaced campaign posters, left over from a previous election?

Similarly, in the second task, it would not be sufficient to decide that distances would be measured from poster to home. Does "home" mean the property line? The front door? A side door which is most often used? The unit of measure must also be specified and uniform throughout the study. The researchers also would have to solve such problems as whether to count a car making a U-turn in front of the observer once or twice.

For each of the tasks and subtasks, the materials column should list all the needed supplies, such as photographs or drawings to aid in identifying the items to be counted, measuring instruments, maps or diagrams of relevant points, and mechanical counting devices or tally sheets.

In addition to the items that you *will* need, you should also provide things that you might need under certain circumstances. These supplies fall into the category of safety precautions: extra copies of printed materials for participants who lose or mislay theirs, electric extension cords to make sure that the tape recorder or mimeograph machine can be plugged into even the most inconvenient socket, extra bulbs for the projector, pencils to use if the rain makes it impossible to write on the slick paper in ink. Even with careful preplanning, however, there will be occasion for improvisation. One researcher remembers a field meeting when the cord of the necessary film projector failed by several feet to reach the only electric outlet in the room. How smug she felt as she pulled the extra cord out of the supply box, and how chagrined, a moment later, to discover that the plugs of the cords could not be mated. Fortunately, a research assistant from another country had had experience with such problems. A paper clip was quickly bent into shape to join the terminals, a roll of packing tape provided insulation, and the project went on. Needless to say, equipment on future field trips was inspected beforehand, and proper fit assured.

Many of the things you need, however, do not fall into

the class of ordinary office or laboratory supplies. For each project, you must identify, locate, and obtain all the things that are peculiar to your study. These may be instruments; raw materials for processing under controlled conditions; special lights or recordings of sounds; or questionnaires, rating forms, instructions, illustrations, and other printed papers.

There is rarely only one way in which the tools can be constructed. Data collection instruments are usually made of ordinary materials, and these materials can be arranged and used in many different ways, colors, shapes, and sizes which have little effect on the research design but which may have dramatic impact on the research process.

Although it seems obvious that materials should be easy and pleasant to use, in fact these issues are often not even considered. Consequently, papers may be printed illegibly, insufficient space provided for responses on forms, or inadequate light provided for reading or examining printed materials. Study materials, of course, should be tried out under actual field conditions if possible. Where it is not possible, deliberate efforts should be made to replicate the field situation, for the purpose of testing the instruments. The test should evaluate both the material itself and its suitability to be used as intended. For instance, the stereotype of the field researcher shows him holding a clipboard, pencil in hand. Clipboards are indeed very useful, but many researchers appear to have neglected their construction. The clip, designed to hold papers in position for writing, is usually at the top of the board. A questionnaire printed in booklet form, on both sides of the paper, must be unfastened and replaced as each page is turned, at some cost in time and convenience. When clipboards are used outdoors or under crowded conditions, the awkward juggling of board, papers, pencils, and any display materials can be seriously distracting. Problems of this type can be foreseen and corrected during a try-out period. There are times, however, when unexpected difficulties occur. Some examples:

At the conclusion of an orientation program for prospective service agency volunteers, the attendees were to complete an evaluation questionnaire on the program. The agency's brochures, uniform trim, report covers, and the like traditionally utilized an intense shade of blue, which had become identified with its public image. For this reason, the program announcements and tickets were also printed on the blue paper, and it seemed a good idea to use this same paper for the questionnaire. The lighting of the auditorium, however, had been planned for the films which formed a large part of the program. In the dim light at their seats, the attendees found the questions printed on dark paper almost impossible to read. In this instance, an attempt to increase the attractiveness of the setting resulted in interference with the study's aims.

The color of paper or decor can be effective, however, if it is carefully planned. In another situation in which a form was distributed, the researchers realized that the subjects would have many papers in their hands by the end of the session. This time a particular form, to be turned in before the end of the day, was printed on bright yellow paper. Not only did the color call attention to itself during the meeting, but team members, standing at the doors as the subjects left, could easily spot the yellow pages and collect them before the group dispersed.

Not only color, but size and shape of materials must be fitted to the study's context. In a recent investigation on food service facilities at a marine corps base, these questions had to be solved. As part of the study, several hundred enlisted men and women were asked to keep complex food diaries, listing all foods eaten during the study period, the times of meals, the locations of the meals (whether they were at home, at a restaurant or fast-food service counter, or somewhere else), and the distances and modes of travel to and from these meals. Since the marines' training schedules allowed them to visit the research site only occasionally, the researcher suggested that the subjects enter the information in pocket notebooks before transferring it to the permanent record forms. The researcher checked with the marine corps and was assured that the marines could carry the notebooks in their uniform pockets, although—because of the traditional regulation that no nonmilitary objects could appear on the uniform—the books had to be covered by the pocket flaps.

The researcher then telephoned the marine corps recruiter in her home city to ask about the pockets on a marine uniform. The recruiter was obviously surprised by the inquiry but provided information on the dimensions of dress and work uniform pockets. The size of the diary could be planned to fit the pockets. The color of its cover was another matter. The researcher wanted the diary to be noticeable when the subject emptied his or her pockets at night or dressed in the morning. At the same time, colors that were too garish or exotic might be considered in bad taste. Because other marine corps forms made use of bright red and yellow, these colors were also eliminated. A bright gold was finally chosen, to provide contrast with the predominantly olive drab and camouflage colors of the uniform.

Procurement

During planning and pretesting, you will have the opportunity to select and try out the materials that will be needed. Some of these materials will be easily available. Measuring devices and equipment used in previous studies may be on hand or purchasable from a nearby supply house. More often, however, the supplies to be used must be designed and manufactured especially for the study. The specifications for instruments and forms are part of the design and will have been determined early in the procedures. Having these items made or printed is another matter. The parent organization may require competitive bids, a time-consuming requisition and purchasing procedure, or justification for obtaining anything outside the regular sources of supply. You should investigate these points very early in the planning process. It is disheartening to be told, five days before your work is to start, that the university's printing plant takes ten days to bind your workbooks or that the special photographic plates you must have are back-ordered at the regional supplier and you must have authorization by the comptroller to purchase them at a retail outlet.

Part of your planning, then, must include accurate information on where items can be obtained, what the proper procedures are for ordering them, and an accurate estimate of how much time is required to obtain them. Once this information is on hand, it must be entered, in reverse order, in your operations schedule. That is, to determine when you must take steps to procure an item, you will count the time backward from the date when the item is needed. An example:

As part of a study of consumer expenditure, all members of a sample of families were requested to keep records of everything on which money was spent, either as purchases or payment for service. In order to keep these records, each family member over 12 years old was asked to carry a small pocket notebook, entering the item or service purchased and the total spent by date and time. The notebooks were designed by the researcher, with spaces for each day of the week, and were to be produced by the printing department of the parent university. The final approval for the booklet format and wording, however, had to come from the agency sponsoring the study, and that approval might be delayed. The printing foreman provided suggestions on how the notebooks could be reproduced and made an acceptable estimate of the cost. Although he would not guarantee delivery by a certain date, he estimated twelve working days to produce the booklet, counting from the date the copy was received by the printer. Since this seemed a very long time, the researcher asked some questions and was told that about four of these days would be required to obtain the paper from the supplier, while at least one more day would go into printing and cutting the covers of the notebooks. Since there was no question about the content of the cover, and the paper could be selected ahead of time, the researcher had the cover printed and the paper ordered in advance. When approval came from the agency, it required only seven workdays to complete the notebooks.

Possible sources of supply at the research site also should be noted. You may discover that you have underestimated the amount of material you will need or that problems you did not anticipate will require different items. These may be no further away than the nearest bookstore or laboratory supply house, but not every community has these amenities open when you need them. The emergency trip for some essential becomes much less traumatic when you have previously scouted out the most convenient supplier. This is not always a commercial outlet. For example:

Interviewers on a survey were being trained at a newly established field office in a small lumbering community. The office was located in the business district, surrounded by stores and a number of restaurants and bars. The first training session lasted until late in the evening, and the trainees were to return at 8:00 the next morning to complete their preparation. As they said good night, the field supervisor happened to mention some materials for the next day's program and discovered that the trainees had not received a packet of these forms which had been mailed to them several days earlier. The trainees went home, and the training team was left with the problem of replacing the missing materials before morning. They had brought a few extra copies, but the office supply shop which did duplicating was closed; and the library, which also had a copying machine, also was closed. There was, however, a coin-operated copier in the lobby of the post office, open all night. A quick tour of the neighboring bars produced $26 in dimes, and the team hurried to the post office. There, feeding in the coins for one page at a time, they duplicated a sufficient number of pages to start the next day's work. In the morning, the remainder of the pages were copied at the store. After that experience, the research team made sure that the supply box for field studies always contained a few rolls of coins for emergency use.

Distribution

From whatever source, you have gathered what you need for the work. All these materials must be organized, packed, and transported to the research site. The packing should allow for a rational arrangement: materials for each part of the project packed together, in the order that they will be used; duplicate supplies packed in different boxes, to guard against having all of a particular supply lost; the management supplies (desk, office, and documentation materials) placed where they can be reached immediately upon arrival. Remember to plan in advance for the end of the project. Supplies should include materials for repacking and returning the tools you have worked with, as well as for protecting and delivering the data which are the reason for the study.

To as great an extent as possible, items should be prepackaged in sets, so that all of the materials required for a particular phase or operation can be handled as a single packet or bundle. What goes into the packet, and the order in which it is arranged, depends on your plan. For example, fifteen interviewers were to be trained during a meeting at a community center. The training agenda listed three types of activities: general training, specific study training, and the completion of office and payroll procedures. The following materials were needed for each of these activities:

General training	*Specific training*	*Office/payroll*
Training manual (mailed to participants in advance)	Study interview schedule	Applications
	Study instructions	Employment papers
Practice interview schedules (3 versions)	Pen	Pen
	Response cards	Travel vouchers for applicant signature
Pen	Illustrations	
Sample ID and introductory materials	Identification badge	Insurance applications
	Introductory letter	
Name tag		Information for employees

The instructions for preparing the packets were as follows:

Materials, Supplies, and Suppliers

Packet A— *General Trng (15)*	*Packet B—* *Specific Trng (15)*	*Packet C—* *Office*
(9×12 manila envelopes—place one at each seat according to table plan)	(12×15 manila envelopes—set out during coffee break)	(have ready at desk —pick up at personnel division)
Practice form 1* (2 copies)	Annotated study schedule (1)	Applications (20)
Practice form 2 (1 copy)	Additional study schedules (2)	Employment forms (20)
Practice form 3 (1 copy)	Instruction (1)	Insurance applications
Response cards for form 3	Response cards (2 sets)	Insurance brochures
Pen	Illustrations (2 sets)	Travel vouchers
Name tag (clipped to outside of envelope)	Badge, ID letters (2)	New employee booklets
Sample ID letter	Introductory letters (2)	
Sample introductory letters (#s 14, 15, 18)		

*Practice forms, cards, sample letters in training file. Name tags, badges, pens, etc., in office supply cabinet downstairs.

    The staff member assigned to the job of preparing the packets could quickly assemble them from the lists and set them out at the proper times during the meeting. The trainees were not distracted by handing around materials and did not have to shuffle unneeded supplies to find what they were to use during each phase. Both leader and members could concentrate on the particular item under discussion.

    Whatever processing you decide to do at the site will also require some materials. These may be tally sheets to record numbers of items reported, labels for marking the units into which different classes of data are separated, or boxes or envelopes for sorting and storing results. The supplies for these operations should be included with the management materials available for use as soon as the data begin to appear. Very early in the research design, you will have planned how the data are to be handled. These plans should be reviewed in light of the setting where the work is to be done, and any necessary changes should be made immediately.

Researchers often find themselves, at some point in the project, suddenly inundated with data. The mechanical facilities for handling these must be ready. There must be staples in the stapler, marking pens for identifying sets of items, labeled boxes in which to place data so that the results of different experimental conditions do not become mixed or misplaced. If the researchers are to maintain control of the operation, the essential sorting and storing activities must keep up with the generation of data.

Gifts and Rewards

In some studies, gifts or rewards to the participants must also be obtained and distributed. Few people question the color or design of money. Other tokens, however, must be selected to please the recipients' taste, which might be very different from the researchers'. When the gift is also intended to reinforce some aspect of the study, its choice may be even more difficult.

Gifts do not need to be large or expensive. A notebook and pen marked with the sponsoring organization's logo might be very acceptable; at the same time, they can remind the participants to keep the records which the project is collecting. In this case, the token serves also as a tool of the research. Here the principal criterion would be its effectiveness. Something seen simply as a reward must meet other standards. Researchers tend to be better educated and more knowledgeable about the arts than subjects are. A picture or object which is pleasing to the participant might be rejected by the researchers, while their choice may find little favor among individuals from other cultural or ethnic backgrounds. An example:

Residents of predominantly working-class neighborhoods were enlisted as panel members in an investigation of the utilization of health care facilities. Those who completed the entire project, by attending a series of meetings and maintaining a three-month-long health report, were to be given a gift. The university-based researchers decided to offer the participants their choice of one of a number of books on health care or a colorful chart of foods and nutrition information. The intent was to link the reward with the subject of the study, but it occurred to one of the team that some of the participants might be uninterested in reading or food chemistry; therefore, an alternative choice of a historical picture of the region was also offered. Almost as an afterthought, one of the staff members suggested still another gift, a 3-by-5-foot American flag, complete with eagle finial and staff. This last choice provided considerable amusement to the more academically oriented researchers, until the gift request forms began to come in. None of the panel members asked for a book, and only one or two wanted the chart as a kitchen decoration. A few selected the picture, but the requests for flags quickly exhausted the local dealer's supplies. Deliveries fell far behind requests, and the gift, planned as a goodwill gesture, resulted in irritation and disappointment as the panel members waited weeks for their gifts. Special orders for flags increased the estimated costs considerably. Fortunately, the books could be returned to the suppliers for refund. The leftover pictures and charts decorated the researchers' offices for some time, as a reminder that the recipients' wishes should be consulted even when the tokens are free.

Food and Lodging

Feeding and housing field workers also comes under the heading of supply. The distinction between the cost of providing food and lodging and other cost factors is an illusionary one. Staff members must eat and sleep. If you do not provide these services, you must pay your workers enough, in money or other goods, to enable them to feed and house themselves. Deciding on whether or not to supply meals and hotel rooms must be done in light of the extent to which your decision affects the work. Sometimes the choice is easy. If you transport a group of interviewers to a distant mining camp for a week, you will also have to arrange for their maintenance there. Similarly, if your researchers are engaged in continuous data collection at a public ceremony and cannot interrupt their work to go out for lunch, you may have to deliver sandwiches to them. In other instances, maximum freedom should be allowed. Field staff members and subjects are most likely to choose to spend off-duty time together. They share a common interest in the research activities and may have other associations which lead them to enjoy each other's company. If the study design does not require any limitation on contact between subjects and researchers, their friendly communication can do nothing but good. Only if the study demands that contacts and information among the study participants be controlled is it necessary to interfere with how and where they interact. Under these circumstances, you may wish to set up separate dining areas, make lounges and bedrooms off-limits to one group or another, or stipulate in great detail which restaurants your staff may patronize. It is easiest to control these activities when food and lodging are supplied as part of the research setting. A related issue is that of how much control you wish to exert over the way in which staff members live in the field. Will they be required to have their meals together? Are they all to be placed in adjoining rooms at the motel?

The amount of togetherness you stipulate should be related to considerations of study management. If the luncheon is a continuation of the meeting, it is reasonable to expect that all attendees will sit together in the dining room. If the conference is situated at an isolated resort hotel, the cocktail hour, small-group discussions, and informal evening get-togethers are probably extensions of working time. Allowing members of the research team to go home at 5:00 p.m. would eliminate valuable data collection activities. You may have to schedule staff time so that no subject is ever out of the presence of a researcher. When such close contact is not essential, however, there are strong arguments in favor of at least occasional separation between observer and observee. Field research is an intense experience. The field staff are constantly under the stress of maintaining the standards of scientific research in strange places. It is exhausting, and an opportunity for relaxation and recuperation is frequently needed. The various demands which subjects and ad hoc staff members make on researchers are not excessive in individual terms, but in combination they can put extremely heavy personal pressure on the primary researchers. It is difficult to obtain privacy in the field. A room of your own, and an evening away from the strain of responding to everyone, permits you to gain perspective on the work. The calm control which the researchers maintain over the chaotic process of field operations is their single most important contribution to success.

Services, such as telephone and transportation, are also part of the materials that must be provided. Installation of and access to telephones, duplicating machines, computer terminals, and similar facilities must be planned and implemented at an early stage. Arrangements with suppliers may require considerable waiting time, including separate delays for installation even after the equipment is delivered to the site.

Transportation raises somewhat different problems. You will be responsible for bringing all the needed people to where they must be and dispatching them to other locations as the fieldwork demands. These tasks may range from simply counting drivers and cars to make sure that everyone can get from here to there to solving intricate routing problems involving multiple transportation modes over long series of connections. Familiarity with bus schedules, taxi rate tables, airline reservation procedures, and the driver's licensing criteria for neighboring states may be required, and this information must be available. You may find it desirable to run a carpool or bus service to assure the presence, on time, of staff members and subjects. When staff or subjects are left to make their own travel arrangements, it is necessary to monitor these arrangements on a continuing basis if the field activities are to progress smoothly. You, or someone to whom you delegate the responsibility, must manage to have all needed people appear at the proper time.

Eight

Documentation

◆◆◆◆◆◆◆◆◆◆◆◆◆◆◆◆◆◆◆◆◆◆◆◆◆◆◆◆◆◆◆◆◆◆◆

Documentation for field research begins as soon as the project is planned. Study design; instruments; correspondence with participants, sponsors, and subject populations; specifications; cost estimates and receipts —all form part of the body of records that you will maintain until the project is completed and reported. Documentation naturally falls into three distinct forms: records of what you plan to do (design, proposals, scheduling); records of what you actually do (field notes, changes in procedures, and the description of methodology which becomes part of your final report); and, finally, the practical records of how you did your work— the expense vouchers, receipts, employment papers for staff members, lists of supplies purchased, and all the other details required for accounting and management purposes. The records should be kept in written form and should be organized and

141

stored so that you can easily refer to any particular item. Above all, they must be complete and comprehensible to an unfamiliar reader—or to you after the details of the event that generated the record have faded from your memory. You will establish a working file from these materials, both to facilitate the ongoing activities and to assist you in preparing reports on the project.

Planning Documents

Your project plan and schedule are themselves documents. The research questions which your study is designed to answer should be stated clearly at the beginning. You must be explicit about what you are looking for, so that you can later determine whether you have found it. Researchers who start out unsure of their goal rarely arrive. The first document in your file, then, should be a clear statement of the study's purpose. It can be as simple as "This study is designed to test the hypothesis that the relationship between owner and employees of small businesses varies systematically with the ethnic characteristics of the owner." It can be, of course, and often is much more elaborate, but an essential element must be the identification of the question which will be asked. Field research frequently produces descriptive, rather than predictive, data. When this is the intention, the research questions can be deemphasized, since the study may have the precise purpose of simply reporting a particular social interaction or condition. An example of this type of research would be the classic anthropological field project, in which a trained investigator observes and records events as they occur in the society under study. Medical case studies are also of this type. When you hope to draw conclusions from your data, or generalize them to other situations, however, there must be a basic structure in the form of a hypothesis. The research statement for the study relating business management and ethnicity also contains the definition of the subjects (owners of specified ethnicity and employees of small businesses) and implicit specifications for the work that will have to be done (identify and measure the relevant indicators of relationship).

The information on what you want to find, who can provide the data, and what has to be done is the basis for constructing your operations schedule. The schedule becomes a part of the file, along with any other materials that you will need in order to set up your work. These may be supplementary references which add to your knowledge, correspondence with other researchers or subject groups, or any other written records. The emphasis in this sentence is on the word *written*. You must record your plans in a permanent form—write notes on your telephone calls or conversations, label calculations and figures, identify photographs and diagrams—as soon as possible. Do not make the common mistake of assuming that you will remember some bit of information because it is important to you. In the stress of fieldwork, it is very common to forget details, to jot down notes without indications of when or to whom they were written, and to make hasty decisions on urgent problems which are never recorded. You should set a regular time each day, or at specific points in the course of the study, to review your notes and to amplify and correct them before they are added to the project file. The cost estimates you have projected and the budget you develop also become a part of this file, along with information on the sources of the money you will use and how it will be accounted for and paid. If you plan to finance your work yourself, the details on funding may be unimportant. Nevertheless, you should make explicit, at the beginning, how the bills are to be paid.

The planning documents tell you what should be done in specific detail, with the tasks operationally described. As the study goes on, you will be able to verify that each task has been completed by checking progress along a series of benchmarks which you will establish. These indicator points may be based on the quantity of work accomplished, the time periods that have elapsed, or the amount of money spent. Which you choose depends on the characteristics of the study. A project that calls for a certain number of hours of activity will be measured by time; one in which the purpose is the collection of a given amount of data will have as its progress indicator some measure of quantity. Whatever the indicator, during the course of the fieldwork you should maintain records that can provide you with information on what has been done and how much is left to do.

The project file should also contain copies of all of the information provided to subjects, the public, and the research staff. These materials should be dated and should carry an indication of how they were disseminated. Letters and other information which you receive should also be noted with the date of receipt. These records verify not only that information was made public but also the content of what was publicized.

The operations schedule is the basic document. You may use the list of tasks it contains to guide the work, or you may translate the list into a graphic form which will clarify the actual steps to be followed. Two types of explicit work instructions are flowcharts and timelines. Both flowcharts and timelines emphasize the specific actions that are to take place, broken down into the discrete operations they require. A flowchart acts as a map through the tasks, plotting the progression through each to the final stage. Each type of operation can be symbolized by the shape of the entry. Conventional symbols are rectangles to indicate an operation; circles, for connection to other operations; diamonds, to show where decisions are to be made; and rhomboids, for statements of information. Remember that the flowchart usually does not differentiate between people. There must be a separate set of instructions for each person or group, clearly indicating which operations on the chart are to be done by each person. The lines connecting the operations indicate direction but not duration. That is, there is no standardized time unit per inch of line. Figure 10 shows a flowchart for a simple field research task.

A timeline also sets out the tasks in order, but it does so in the context of a time schedule. To prepare a timeline, first

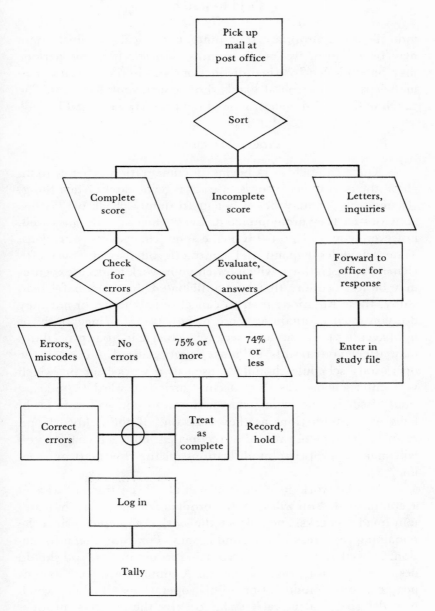

Field Office Operations: Test Score Processing

Figure 10. Sample Flowchart

indicate the appropriate time units, in vertical columns. These may be minutes, weeks, or months; and specific time periods may be exploded for finer distinctions within the overall schedule. Separate horizontal bands show concurrent activities. The timeline for a field operation might appear as in Figure 11.

Progress Documents

Once the fieldwork begins, documentation expands to include the day-to-day records of what is being done. When things go smoothly, it may be sufficient to simply check off various activities as they are completed. Even when a study goes well, however, you will probably make some changes in your plans. Time schedules expand and contract; you may discover efficiencies in operations, which lessen your work load; or expenses may be less or more than you anticipated. In a successful field study, these variations tend to cancel out. Whether or not they do, you must maintain a record of how things change, both for bookkeeping purposes and because a change in your procedures may affect your results and must be rationalized. A copy of the operations schedule should be used as a worksheet on which you enter changes as they occur, carried forward to indicate their effect on succeeding stages. Here too you will note problems or contradictions as they arise out of the fieldwork and record how they are solved or reconciled. For each change, you will make appropriate modifications on the flowchart or timeline.

As the work goes on, you will also keep track of what is accomplished. You will tally the products of the research, maintain quality checks, and balance the work completed against the remaining resources of time and money. For your own information, as well as to meet any reporting requirements, you should design a form for progress reports. A simple form for this purpose can be a modification of the operations schedule, which provides space, after each task, to enter the progress information. The staff members who will be responsible for monitoring

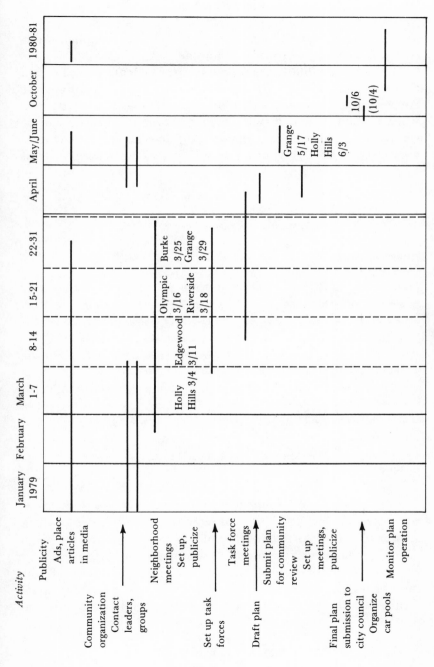

Figure 11. Shoreline Community Plan Citizens' Participation Evaluation

and supervising activities also must have clear and explicit directions for keeping the records required.

Examine your plans to identify the contingent tasks; that is, those that cannot be done until something else is completed. An immediate purpose of the progress report is to notify you when the antecedent task is finished. Your report form can be standardized to facilitate entering up-to-date information, at regular intervals as Figure 12 shows. Quick comparison of items

Figure 12. Sample Report Form

Skill Mastery Teaching Program Evaluation

Progress Report Through _____ School _____

Children tested this month _____	Booklets completed this month	_____
Children tested to date _____	Booklets completed to date	_____
a. Percent of total _____%	b. Percent of total _____%	
Booklets evaluated this month _____	Class visits completed this month	_____
Booklets evaluated to date _____	Class visits completed to date	_____
c. Percent of total _____%	d. Percent of total _____%	

e. Costs this month $ _____

   Costs to date $ _____

f. Percentage of total budget _____   g. Percent toward goal to date _____
   expended to date

f and g provides the immediate information on your progress, while items a through d will allow you to identify areas where greater care or effort should be placed. When the ratio of total cost to total progress toward goal approaches 1, you can be assured that your fieldwork is proceeding successfully. If the time schedule of the study is important, the progress report should also show the proportion of time expended in relation to progress.

Documentation

The records, reports, and other documents interact. Schedules produced to organize the work at the beginning of the project are the structure on which actual progress data are entered; progress summaries, in turn, can become the bases for sections of interim and final reports.

Reports

The final product of your research will probably be a report in which you present the results of the study. How these data are presented may be inherent in the study design itself; a doctoral dissertation or term paper, for example, will have well-established criteria, as will the yearly report of a service agency. The information you collect on procedures and progress is likely to figure only peripherally in a report of this type. During the course of the study, you will need other information. The progress data which you collect will be used to prepare field reports. Field reports serve at least two purposes. They provide management information to you on the status of your project; they also inform others about what is being done in the field. The report may be informal and casual, such as a telephone call from a coworker to say that a particular task has been completed; or it may be highly detailed and stringently presented. The obligation to deliver a progress report at fixed intervals during the study may be explicit in your contract or agreement to do the work. Even when you have made no such commitment, it is a good idea to prepare a progress report. You must assume at least a minimal interest on the part of sponsors, coworkers, and subjects. Having invested time, effort, or money in your research, they deserve to know what has happened to their contribution. A progress report distributed to coworkers and sponsors can serve a number of important functions. It can be used to maintain interest in your work and encourage cohesion among staff members. Figure 13 shows what a weekly memo to field workers might contain.

149

Field Research

Figure 13. Sample Weekly Memo

South County Service Area
Handicapped Children's Transportation Project
September 16

Memo to interviewers and drivers:

1. The end of August saw the completion of data collection in 270 households, almost 65 percent of our total. Congratulations! Despite the early delays caused by the miserable weather in spring, we are maintaining our field schedule. The health department has agreed to give us time during the state meeting, October 4, to present a summary of our results so far. Carl Evans will be contacting several drivers to arrange for filming the pickup at some homes. We'll show the films at the meeting, as we discuss the study. The field staff is welcome to attend.

2. Barbara Ryan in the field office has asked interviewers to be especially careful in filling out their weekly time sheets. Remember that you must enter the ID number of every household you visit, along with the date and time. Correcting incomplete time sheets has delayed payroll clearance several times this summer.

3. Please note the following corrections:
   Change in activity code, page 6:
   Two additional categories of games have been added.
   (1) If the child plays cards, chess, checkers, Monopoly, etc., *with siblings,* enter this on line 23, as "Other." Games played with parents or grandparents should continue to be listed under "Family," line 14.
   (2) *Recreational swimming* should be shown separately. Swimming as therapy should be entered on page 4, recreational swimming on page 6.

Thank you all for your help. Remember to check with your supervisors when you are ready for new assignments.

The form in which progress reports are made may be dictated by some sponsoring agency, with explicit instructions as to how items are to be listed or totals summarized. A study conducted under less restrictive controls, however, still must be reported. If you work by yourself, or under only nominal control by an instructor or supervisor, you will have even greater need for complete records. You will not have the support services of an institution to keep your books and generate your interim reports. A reporting form designed for your own use can organize the field data into the way most useful for your own operations. To set up such a system, you must first decide what kinds of reports you will need and in what order the data should be

150

presented. The operations schedule is the obvious place to begin. It will suggest the logical points at which reports should be made, such as at the completion of a particular phase or regularly spaced over some intervals of time or effort.

Early in the project, you should decide who will get field reports, so that the appropriate distribution is maintained throughout the fieldwork. Certainly. the sponsors of a funded study should be kept informed, as should the supervisor or instructor who is responsible for monitoring your work. Co-workers may be aware of progress through their participation; where they are not, you must be sure to provide them with the information. Their ability and willingness to schedule their efforts will be related directly to their knowledge about the status of the work. Subjects may or may not be informed, depending on what effect the report would have on their contribution. At the end of the study, of course, it may be highly desirable to prepare a summary of results for the subjects, to provide them with a sense of closure and some idea of how what they did fitted into the project.

Maintaining the Documents

At the end of the fieldwork, you must decide what to do with the papers that have been accumulated. Some of them may be incorporated directly into the final report you will prepare, either in the body of the report or as technical appendices. The contents of other materials in the file may be summarized or paraphrased. In both of these cases, original documents which are not raw data can be discarded if you are sure that there will be no further need to refer to them in reporting on or planning further work. However, you cannot always be sure that they will not be needed again. Later research may throw new light on your findings, or your conclusions may be challenged; consequently, you may need to reexamine your original data long after you have completed your study. You will want to retain important materials, but there are rational limits to what you can store. The attics and closets of research institutions are stuffed with papers referring to studies long forgotten. Even if extensive storage space is available, the sheer mass of paper generated in the course of research activities makes it almost impossible to sort out and identify the specific items which will be needed. You should set a time, at the end of your fieldwork, to review your files, condense and organize them, and dispose of the excess.

What is it safe to throw out? You can discard, to begin with, duplicates of any materials. During the fieldwork, you will have held copies of the schedules, work assignments, tests, sample lists, and other working records, so that you could replace anything which was lost and maintain control over what was going on. At the end of the study, you probably retrieved the originals, either turned in as reports on work done or inspected to verify results. Once you have transcribed any special information onto your master copies of these materials, the field copies can be discarded. A number of separate scoring sheets or tallies can be condensed to one complete record. You will certainly want to retain the raw data, but there is no real need to keep more than one processed set. You should hold the card deck, or tape, or printouts, but not all three. You will want to keep at least a few copies of unused forms, blank questionnaires, tests, maps, and pictures. You will probably find, when all the field materials are collected, that there are substantial quantities of supplies which were scattered in various hands. Most of these can be recycled or thrown out.

Besides duplicates, you can discard undeveloped records, such as rough notes or preliminary reports already written up in final form. What should not be discarded are the business and management records of employment and expenditures and formal agreements with subjects, staff members, and sponsors. Correspondence should be evaluated. If the letter says "Dear Joe, Thanks for meeting me at the center. I enjoyed our talk. Regards, Fran," there is probably no need to keep it, unless you foresee that at some time you will want some documentation of the meeting. A similar letter which adds "I agree that the data are strong confirmation of the thesis. In my opinion, you should report the results directly to the institute. See Hanson, and tell her that we'll continue after the holidays" carries substantive information and should be kept.

In one form or another, many of the study materials will become a part of the final report. Consider the roles which various documents played in the following example:

Three students in a course in organizational psychology chose to cooperate in writing a term research paper on the cultural aspects of management style. Two of the students were Asian-Americans familiar with the small family-owned grocery stores, laundries, and drug stores in the city's International District. They suggested studying the relationships between ethnicity and management in a sample of Japanese, Chinese, Filipino, and white-owned businesses, matched for gross income, number of employees, and length of operation under the same owner. The final product of their research would be the term papers on which their course grades would be based. Besides these documents, what other types of records would be generated and utilized in the study?

First, of course, the investigators had to design their study. To choose their sample of businesses, they had to identify the appropriate ethnic status of the owners, determine the number of employees and the total amount of income, and obtain the cooperation of the owners. Fortunately, a local directory published by the city's Minority Affairs Commission listed the type of business and name of owner of all stores in the district. In almost all cases, the owner's name was sufficient to indicate ethnicity; in the few cases in which Spanish-sounding Chicano and Filipino names were similar, the Asian students' friends or relatives in the community were able to distinguish between the two. Identifying white-owned businesses was much more difficult and required finally that the researchers visit a number of neighborhoods, walking along shopping streets, reading store signs, and chatting with nearby business people until a list of eligible owners could be developed. The sample lists, together with the criteria for eligibility, became part of the working file.

The state auditor maintained records of the premiums paid by businesses for employee insurance coverage and of the reports submitted for the purpose of calculating the state's Business and Occupation Tax. From these records, open to the public, the students were able to draw their matched samples within each of the ethnic groups. Photocopies of the relevant pages were filed.

A questionnaire was constructed to obtain information on how each owner organized work responsibilities and trained and supervised employees and on how the informal associations of the owners and employees were structured. The instrument was submitted to the class instructor and then pretested on a small number of shops. The original questionnaire, the instructor's comments, the results of the pretest, and the students' evaluation of the questionnaire were placed in the file, along with the revised instrument which was prepared. Meanwhile, the researchers completed their operations schedule and a timeline for the study. A letter, soliciting participation and signed jointly by the instructor and the students, was sent to the store owners. The letter requested that the owner return a card indicating a convenient time for the students to visit the business. The returned cards were filed to demonstrate permission, and the suggested times entered on the timeline. From this, an assignment sheet for each student was developed. The design statement, tested and revised instruments, operations schedule, timeline, sample list, and individual assignment sheets formed the body of planning documents for the study.

The data were collected in visits to the various stores, interviews with owners and employees, and observation of in-store communication during timed periods of operation. It quickly became apparent that the research disrupted business during the more crowded shopping periods, and the schedule was changed to accommodate this problem. Eliminating data collection at these times, however, meant that more field days

Documentation

would be required. The timeline admitted some expansion but not enough to permit the study to be completed before the end of the quarter. The students' instructor agreed to accept their term papers late. She signed the university's late-grade authorization form for each of the students, and the forms were submitted to the registrar's office. The students' copies of the form were added to the study file. The changed dates were entered on the timeline and assignment sheets, also filed. The students had agreed to share the costs of the study and had each contributed $10 to a petty cash fund. One of them was selected to be treasurer. He made up an accounting record on which to note the money spent and asked the other students to give him the receipts for any expenditures. The accounting form was drawn on an envelope, and the receipts and bills were put into the envelope. As each was entered on the form, the treasurer initialed it, to indicate that it had been tallied. The running tally signaled that the $30 was almost exhausted before the end of the field-work, and the students added more money to the fund. The term papers were due two weeks before the end of the quarter. At that date, and again on the day when course grades were calculated, the students submitted a report to the instructor, showing how much of the study was done and when they expected to complete it. The instructor's approval, initialed and dated, was put into the file. Several of the store owners had mentioned the study to the International District chamber of commerce, which asked for more information. A brief summary of the study's design and purpose was prepared, and one of the students presented this summary at a chamber meeting. Her notes, attached to a clipping from the neighborhood newspaper which reported the meeting, were also filed.

The students' term papers received high grades and served as the final report for the study. A single introduction, summarizing the results, was written and distributed to the participants, along with a letter of thanks. The documents in the working file contributed to the report to some extent, providing details of the methodology. A more important point had to do with a question of bias, raised by the instructor. During the course of the study, a series of television programs on cultural diversity in the city had closely examined businesses in the International District. Using their records of permission cards received and dates when the interviews and observations were conducted, the students were able to demonstrate that there were no systematic differences between data collected before the programs and after. The financial records which the treasurer had kept proved to be unexpectedly valuable. The department adviser pointed out that the university had some funds for undergraduate research, and the students applied. Their careful and detailed accounting was accepted, and their money reimbursed. A final benefit of documentation arose when the transcript of one of the students showed a failing grade for the course. She challenged it and was told that no grade or late-grade authorization had been turned in. The copy of the form, found in the study's file, spared her the inconvenience of appealing the grade through the university's cumbersome machinery.

What information can be retained, and how it can be used, is subject to federal and local laws and regulations regarding privacy and the protection of individual rights. Institutions frequently have their own requirements as well. Obtaining permission from subjects does not free you from the obligation to act in accordance with these laws. Unfortunately, there is still considerable ambiguity about how they are to be interpreted and enforced, and the status of the records you may wish to maintain is likely to be unclear. To comply with both the letter and the intent of the law, you would be well advised to include legal consultation at an early stage in your design.

Nine

Managing
Field Operations

◆◆◆◆◆◆◆◆◆◆◆◆◆◆◆◆◆◆◆◆◆◆◆◆◆◆◆◆◆◆◆◆◆◆

As the study continues, issues related to the work in progress must be faced. For example, policies must be set for handling and safeguarding data and field materials; the interactions between staff members and others must be monitored; and methods and procedures must be adapted to changing events and situations.

Managing Materials

Data collected in the field will require some minimal processing in the field before they are returned to the primary work location. At the very least, you will count them, to make sure you have enough of whatever it is that has been collected;

examine them, to make sure that what you have collected meets the criteria that have been defined; and log them in, to record what has been done. How much else is done depends on the resources available and the complexity of the tasks. Simple editing, tallying, or sorting can be done anywhere there is a pencil and a flat surface to work on. The field staff may be able to do much of this preliminary processing. As a matter of fact, such activities may help to occupy their time between scheduled research tasks and will show them how the data they collect must be handled and what problems are caused by unclear or inadequate reports. An interviewer who accepts meaningless terms in answer to a question sees the problem very quickly when she is required to fit the answer into a highly categorized response code, and a staff member who cannot bother to keep accurate records of the time spent on various activities gains a new respect for the directions when it is his responsibility to schedule the work.

Temporary facilities set up in the field do not have to be elaborate. A supply of cartons from the supermarket or liquor store can be labeled to store different categories of materials. The tape, string, and marking pens you bring in your supply boxes can be used to mark off and organize work in different stages of processing. What is important is that the materials be protected and maintained so that errors will not be made when the data are processed. That is, you must make sure that the materials are not damaged, lost, or used out of order. A field office is usually improvised, without optimum facilities for storing and handling the supplies you will use, and with limited access to replacements. Managing materials under these circumstances requires that you institute control procedures for keeping and disbursing them. You may want to set up a logging system which records everything taken out of the supply, ask people to sign out equipment and materials, and make sure that someone is responsible for securing them at the end of the day. Providing special places for each category of material, clearly marked to indicate whether that box contains sharpened pencils or completed tests, is essential. Things should be arranged in some logical order, with materials used at the same time stored together, or a set of booklets to be handed out consecutively stacked in the order in which they will be distributed. When the telephone is ringing, two subjects have just checked in to get their next task, the janitor is calling your attention to the posted notice of closing hour, and your forefinger is caught in the knot of the package you are tying up to send by the next mail, you will not have time to search for the new ID badges, which should be, but are not, in the supply cabinet. Allow yourself time, when setting up your work area, to make rational decisions on where operations should take place and where materials will be most conveniently located. It is a good idea to walk through the activities where they will occur. Even if your office will be the trunk and back seat of your car, there will be better and worse ways of setting it up. It is worth the time to find the best.

Safeguarding Confidentiality

The data must also be protected in another sense. Here the problem is more than the safety of the material in a physical sense. Questions and answers to tests, questionnaire responses, recorded observational reports, films, and tapes require special treatment. From a practical standpoint, you do not want the information from one subject to contaminate that given by another; and you want to make sure that test questions are not published. The precautions you take to lock up or cover the results, the restrictions you place on exposing them to non-authorized people, and the care with which you shield the data during processing are designed to enhance the quality of the research. Your procedures to protect the results, however, also have another purpose. In contributing the data, the subjects, whether they know it or not, have given you the responsibility of protecting their privacy. This is a serious charge and deserves considerable care. For the most part, what the subjects tell you

159

or allow you to observe will not reflect negatively on them. In many cases, however, the subjects place information in your hands which could embarrass or harm them if it were disclosed. They trust you to use it for beneficial purposes. In soliciting their cooperation, you have probably assured them that their contributions would be held in confidence. You must make every effort to do this. When confidentiality is breached or subjects' identities exposed, it is usually through carelessness rather than intention. Researchers tend to become casual about the data they collect; after having interviewed 200 teenagers about marijuana use, they may find it hard to remember that to each respondent the admission is a real risk in a personal sense, with very real negative consequences possible. The guidelines and regulations for the protection of human subjects which universities, public agencies, and institutions are increasingly enforcing set strict standards for the safeguarding of data. You must build the protection into your procedures from the beginning.

You may want to provide a separate facility for storing materials which must be secured. They may be placed in a locked file, or stored in a different room, or kept by a researcher who is not associated with your project. As the individual responsible for the conduct of the fieldwork, you must make the arrangements for delivery of the data to their storage place and authorize access by appropriate people. You will probably be the one who has the information linking subjects' names with their data; if the link is blind-coded, you will have the key to the code. Having this information makes you accountable for its safety.

At the conclusion of the study, you must arrange for the disposition of the data and of any identifying information. Unless you have obtained explicit permission from the subjects to use their names or identify them, this information should be destroyed immediately. It may sound melodramatic, but many researchers make a point of burning such information, usually in the presence of a witness. Many universities and research institutions have procedures for shredding or burning records

Managing Field Operations

and will provide a witness and a certification of the destruction for the record. The data, either anonymous or with the subjects' permission, can then be prepared for processing and analysis.

Personal Safety and Security

Of necessity, some fieldwork will be done under conditions of risk. Studies are conducted in ghettos, in conflict situations, among people who are under stress, and in areas where cultures clash. Researchers who enter such situations may lack the necessary survival skills. Even when they are alerted to potential dangers, they may be forced by the requirements of the project to expose themselves. It is your responsibility to provide the greatest degree of protection possible.

Particular areas may be safe or unsafe depending on the time of day. The central areas of many cities, for example, are busy and secure places during the working day but deserted and dangerous after dark. Similarly, areas of a neighborhood vary in safety; while the shops along the street side of a large apartment complex may be crowded with housewives doing their family shopping, the inner courtyards or roofs can be controlled by feuding gangs. Your preliminary study of the site will identify some of these problems, while the first contact with local residents will provide more detailed information. The people in the study area are usually sensitive to dangers and anxious to protect newcomers whom they have decided to accept. The goodwill of the neighborhood is probably the best security you will have. Subjects will warn researchers about dangerous streets and events; they will often volunteer to escort investigators to and from their stations or arrange to meet in places they know to be safe. Sponsorship, or at least acceptance, by local power groups is also important. The researcher who is introduced to an inner-city recreation center by an influential figure in the street society not only will gain subjects but also is much less likely to have her briefcase stolen when she leaves the building. A relationship with a local group or individual can also be a handicap,

161

however. In strongly polarized communities, such an association may shut you out of interactions with opposing groups; you may find yourself the captive of one side in a local struggle for resources or dominance.

For example, the Child Nutrition Program of a city's health and welfare department was asked to report on the dietary enhancement effects of a free breakfast program operated by a volunteer inner-city social center. The study would attempt to measure not only the quality of food served at the center but also any changes in food purchases and use by families of children in the program. The researchers had been told, and believed, that access to the community would be very difficult without assistance, and they welcomed the offer of the center's officials to sponsor the study. At the time, the center was involved in a conflict with several established charities over the right to administer a large amount of money allocated to food distribution by the state. It soon became apparent to the researchers that their findings would be used to support the center's claim to the money, and there was increasing pressure on them to report favorable results. When they refused to exaggerate their findings, cooperation stopped. The researchers were locked out of the center's kitchen and dining room, their supplies were stolen or vandalized, and word was spread on the neighborhood grapevine that talking to the investigators would threaten the welfare payments on which many families existed. One researcher was told that if he remained, he would be "taken care of," and his supply of data collection forms was doused with gasoline and burned to emphasize the warning. The study was salvaged only by two fortunate factors. While waiting for contacts with the community to be established, the researchers had collected a considerable amount of data at the center, sufficient for most of the analyses they needed. And one member of the team had been born and raised in the community; her relationship to several older people still living there, and to a church in the neighborhood, opened other avenues of access to residents. Indeed, many of the families were actually afraid of the center's leaders and participated only after the researchers demonstrated their independence of the more militant group. The study was scaled down and completed with anxiety, but no real harm came to the investigators.

Knowledge about the inner politics and lines of communication within a community, then, is essential. Even with this information, however, researchers may be vulnerable to danger. What protections can be given them? It is important to make it clear to subjects that your investigators have the support of some organization or group and that the organization knows where they will be, whom they will contact, and when they will return. You may wish to send a letter, registered if necessary, to every subject, setting out the details of the researcher's visit. This serves to reassure both the subjects and the researchers; the former know who will call on them, and approximately when, while at the same time the researchers know that the organization is aware of where they will be and that it can be expected to determine whether they arrived safely. For their part, field workers may be required to check in at regular intervals, to report their arrival on the site, and to follow certain specified procedures for traveling safely. Installing safety locks on the door of a field office or using a peep hole before admitting subjects to the workroom might be necessary.

Sometimes the danger arises not out of the research activities themselves but simply because researchers are in an area where dangerous events occur. For instance, in a study designed to develop realistic training materials for city bus drivers, observers were assigned to ride the buses and gather critical incidents of behavior by drivers and passengers. On one central city run, it became apparent to an observer that riders were dealing in drugs during the trip, with buyers and sellers boarding the bus at prearranged stops, conducting their business in the back seats, and separating at the next corner. In this case, the observer's duty as a citizen to report a crime conflicted with the needs of the research, as well as with his self-interest in avoiding the attention of the armed dealers. A second staff member was assigned to ride with the first, to provide some protection and also to make the observer less conspicuous. The incidents were reported to the police at the end of the data collection period.

There are many circumstances when two researchers are safer than one. Women staff members often prefer to be accompanied by their husbands or male friends in the field, and it may be well worthwhile to pay these escorts for their services. Sometimes it is useful to have a guard unobtrusively present. In one study on an isolated military base, for example, it was necessary for women interviewers to visit recreational facilities at night. The base commander, concerned about safety, required that the woman be accompanied by a noncommissioned officer, although the researchers feared that the presence of an observer might inhibit the respondents from candid evaluation. The solution to the problem was to have the noncommissioned officer, wearing off-duty clothes, go to the facility before the interviewer arrived. He was then able to lounge in the background as the interviews were conducted, unnoticed by the respondents. In work on the streets, a second staff member waiting in the car may prevent the vehicle from being vandalized and also enable one researcher to leave the car when a parking space is impossible to find.

Security measures can also work against you, especially in apartments and homes that are guarded against strangers. It may be very difficult to reach a resident to ask for access. Many large apartment buildings in the city have elaborate security systems almost impossible to breach. Locked outer doors and doormen may prevent you from even learning the names of tenants so that you cannot even reach them to request their cooperation. In some cases, an indirect approach can be used. Researchers have waited outside such buildings until residents left for work, followed them to their offices, and sought contacts in their company to effect introductions. A somewhat less dangerous method was tried by an investigator who wished to interview several residents of a guarded condominium near a large medical center. Reasoning that at least some of the tenants would be

164

doctors, the researcher obtained a directory of physicians and identified several whose home addresses fell in the building. She wrote a personal letter to each, explaining the research and asking for assistance. Two physicians responded, and one offered to introduce her to his neighbors. With this entry, she was able to complete her work.

With imagination and care, you will be able to improvise solutions to many problems of safety and security. There is no denying, however, that such problems can seriously impede field research and are likely to become worse. In smaller cities and rural areas, the researcher can still find open doors and a willingness to speak to strangers, but even in these settings there is more suspicion than in the past. In larger cities, the situation is critical. Not only are there very real dangers, but the use of the term *research* to cover high-pressure salesmanship, political campaigning, fraud, and casing the homes of potential burglary victims has placed legitimate investigations in disrepute. Coping with these disadvantages will be among the urgent issues you will face.

Monitoring Interactions

At its best, fieldwork re-creates the relationship of friends, or host and guest, between researcher and subject. At worst, the interaction can be that of an invasion into personal space, resisted with all the fury of guerilla warfare. To begin with, you will have at least nominal authorization to be where you are and to carry out your research activities. It is up to you to translate this situation into one in which willing and enthusiastic cooperation is offered. The minimal requirement is that you give no offense and do no harm. Your research will have been designed to be safe for its participants; making it pleasant is the work of the field staff. You should select the field researchers, including yourself, from among those who like to be with people and can fit comfortably into the society where the study takes place. Researchers, as a rule, are better educated, more sophisticated, and more knowledgeable than their subjects. Even where the field staff members are drawn from the study community, the training received makes them superior to the subjects in the area of the research. You must use your knowledge and skills to manage the work in such a way that the participants will not be patronized or denigrated. Almost by definition, subjects are naive. Basic courtesy demands that you do not insult or take advantage of them.

Not giving offense, however, is a more subtle constraint. People have certain standards of behavior that must not be violated. Common sense will indicate the more obvious problems. In planning your field procedures, you will have noted and allowed for general community behavior levels—under what conditions people of different ages and sexes can swear, for instance, or at what times it is appropriate for women to enter taverns or for men to wear jewelry. You will have briefed the field staff to accommodate to these standards. Individuals have personal definitions of proper behavior, however, which are more difficult to recognize. The best general rule is to let the subject initiate the activities that take place, insofar as possible within the requirements of the research. That is, do not smoke unless invited to do so, wait until the subject indicates a chair before you sit down, and wait until you have some idea of the social dynamics of a group before you begin speaking to any of its members. Failing to take these precautions might mean that an asthmatic respondent cannot complete an interview, an older wife might be made uncomfortable because you are sitting in her husband's customary chair, or you have unwittingly violated the hierarchy of a street gang and thus lost it from your sample. Even more idiosyncratic standards may result in damage to full cooperation. A person who does not like strong perfume will be unwilling to accept an investigator wearing heavy scent. In one instance, an in-depth interview with an executive was cut short because the interviewer's heavy watch bracelet clanked against the desk as he wrote; the noise distracted and irritated the respondent. During another meeting with a public official, the researcher waited while the official read over the introductory materials on the study. While he waited, the researcher amused himself by examining the samples of quartz which decorated the desk top. The official stopped reading, abruptly refused to participate, and ordered the researcher to leave at once. The study was long over when the researcher met a friend who worked in the official's department; only then did he hear about how much the man cherished his ornaments and how furious he became if anyone touched them. Field research does not demand that you maintain constant silence, keep your hands folded in your lap, and dress in somber colors. It does require that you be sensitive to your subjects' preferences and make as few errors as you can. Do not forget that the field is their world, and you are a stranger there. They are likely to act as good hosts, but you must be a good guest.

Coping with the Unexpected

An American humorist once described a magnificent birthday banquet, during which a uniformed crew of singing boatmen were to row a decorated barge across the flooded ballroom floor, bearing a cake surmounted by lighted candles to the dais where sat the guest of honor. Just as the barge reached the foot of the steps, it overturned, dropping cake, candles, and singing boatmen into the water before the astonished guests. Instantly, from behind a curtain, an identical barge appeared, its similarly dressed singing crew carrying a duplicate of the cake safely to its intended recipient. The resourceful hotel manager, who had thus prepared for any eventuality, would have made an excellent director of field research.

There well may be investigations which justify preparations of this magnitude. Studies involving extremely rare populations or transient events, such as interviews with aged representatives of lost cultures or research on the immediate effects of disasters, might call for duplication of all of the investigative tools you need or even more heroic steps. Media preparations for coverage of events or appearances of importance—such as the provision of supplementary cameras and reporters, commentators at separate sites, and background or filler material to be broadcast from the studio—are examples of the efforts which can be made to assure that the occasion will not be lost, even if some machines or people fail to complete their tasks. For the most part, your research will not require such elaborate preparations. What you must do, however, is make some accurate estimates of the effect and cost of equipment and/or staff failure and of the costs involved in insuring yourself and your project against these losses.

Providing the mechanisms which protect you against loss requires, first, that you evaluate the potential damage to the project which each type of failure might do to your overall plan. Next, you should try to determine how these failures can be avoided and at what cost. In planning terms, this calculation is often referred to as a crash plan, an advance determination of what can be done to minimize loss or retrieve success when things go wrong.

There is no limit to the number and strength of the backup or fail-safe mechanisms which can be built into the project. With sufficient attention and resources, you can ensure against virtually any threat from accident or error. Each protective element, however, carries some cost, either in time or money or in a loss of spontaneity and rhythm in process. Taking into account these needs and their associated costs, you must decide which backup mechanisms are economically defensible. Ordering enough extra pencils to allow for those which will be thoughtlessly broken during the stress of the project is an obvious precaution. Deciding precisely how many subjects a single researcher can manage in group activities is more complex, and the stakes are correspondingly higher. Supplying too many pencils would cause only minor problems of cost and handling. Extra boxes could probably be returned to the supplier, and their weight and bulk would add little to the effort of the study. Running out of pencils in the midst of the experiment, on the other hand, might be a major embarrassment. In this circumstance, there are few arguments against providing more pencils than your original plan strictly calls for. Allocation of more expensive units, such as people, requires greater thought. Recruiting, training, supervising, and rewarding people are activities too important to expend on those who are not necessary to the project. Too few staff members or an unscheduled toothache in an essential participant, however, can seriously threaten a project. Along with the statement of needed resources which appears in your plan, then, you should also have estimates of how flexible these needs are, and how, if necessary, people and materials could be shifted to cover unexpected gaps. An example:

As part of a study of group decision making, delegates to a church conference agreed to permit a team of researchers to design the procedures by which the conference would consider a number of proposed modifications to vestry authority. The research called for the delegates to meet in small groups under one of four different types of committee structure. Members would be assigned roles as proposer, moderator, discussant, or analyst. They would receive their assignments, and information on where their group would meet, at a central desk each morning. The group discussions would be monitored by observers, who would record the interactions among members. Based on a Graeco-Latin Square design, each delegate would be rotated through all roles and all structure types on each question. The groups would meet each day around small tables in hotel meeting rooms. Under some of the structure types, starting and stopping times would be strictly adhered to, while others were more informal. The conference leadership and the delegates were cooperative and interested in the study, which they believed would assist them in improving lay participation in church affairs. They were, however, not sophisticated about research and could not be expected to understand the importance of following exact design specifications. The operations schedule for the field components of this study appears in Figure 14. As it indicates, the investigators had made elaborate plans for the work. What could go wrong with this study, and how could errors be corrected?

The procedures were explained to the delegates at a preliminary meeting. Unfortunately, this session was scheduled to follow an earlier set of committee meetings among regional officials, which ran overtime. At the hour scheduled for the subjects' meeting, then, not all of the participants were there; and, as the delay continued, some of the early arrivals drifted off to chat with friends, visit the coffee shop, or attend to other affairs. Even after announcements over the loudspeaker system, and messengers sent to various public areas to call in stragglers, the investigators suspected that some members of the group were still absent. The exact number could not be verified, however, since on this first day of the meetings there still was no complete count of the delegates and other attendees. Despite this problem, the instructions were given, and the members of the group who planned to participate in the next day's meetings were also given a mimeographed booklet containing the step-by-step procedures to be followed. At this time, however, two changes were made. The conference secretary announced that a sightseeing excursion for guests and members had been rescheduled for the following afternoon, and a room conflict discovered by the hotel necessitated that activities planned for one particular meeting room take place instead in several smaller areas. The participants were asked to make a note of these changes in their programs and in the mimeographed instructional material. The investigators answered questions about the study, repeated their instructions as to the time and places of the first discussions, and the meeting adjourned.

The conference participants went to their dinners and the evening program. In the room occupied by the principal investigator, however, the research team gathered to assess possible problems and to plan how to deal with them. The most obvious was the room change, which meant that a certain number of

Figure 14. Operations Schedule for Church Laity Conference Study

Task	Subtasks	Location	Staff	Materials	Time	Notes
Assign group members	1. Randomly select from list	Office	Ryan, Brant, Stull, Wilkins secretary	Registrant list	Prior to July 25	As soon as list arrives from church headquarters—deadline for sign-up is July 15
	2. Set up schedule			Hotel floor plan, conference program	Prior to July 30	
Instruct delegates	1. Prepare instructional material	Office	Ryan, Brant secretary	Design statement, memo from Rev. Lang on program	Prior to August 1	Send draft to Rev. Lang for review
	2. Brief delegates	Conference (Ballroom?)	Brant		August 11 5:30 p.m.	Have extra copies of all materials for church files
	3. Distribute instructions		All staff	Assignment sheets, description of study		
Morning meetings (all days)	1. Set up meeting rooms	Meeting rooms	As assigned	Assignments, tape recorder, extra tapes, tally sheets	By 8:30 a.m.	Be in room by 8:00 a.m. to greet early arrivals
	2. Check attendance			Master assignment list	9:00–9:15	Send messengers out to find missing discussants
	3. Monitor 1st discussion			Recording and reporting forms	9:15–10:30	
	4. Reshuffle, reorganize 2nd discussion			Master assignment list	10:45–12:00	
Afternoon meetings (all days)	(Same organization as mornings, except for time schedule: 1st discussion 1:30–2:45					
	2nd discussion 3:00–4:15)					

discussion groups would be separated from immediate super-vision of the researchers. Added to this difficulty was the state-ment by one of the team that the lush gardens surrounding the hotel seemed to have triggered his latent allergies and that he was already suffering from what he knew from experience would be increasingly serious physical ailments. At the very least, these two factors threatened a significant deficit in the monitoring that was an essential part of the design.

The researchers' ability to cope with these difficulties was limited by still another unexpected factor, the uncertainty about the exact number of participants who would join in the discussions. A casual conversation with one of the conference organizers brought out the fact that many local church mem-bers did not preregister but simply came and entered into the conference activities as they found it convenient. Other dele-gates frequently combined attendance at meetings with visits to friends, shopping, and the like, so that the program committee did not expect to have the entire group present at all scheduled activities, except the formal dinner and worship service. The original plan, to give each participant a complete schedule of his or her discussion assignments on the first morning, had to be abandoned. Instead, the researchers made up a set of assignment sheets, by which participants could be sorted into groups as they arrived and signed in. This meant, however, that the rota-tion of participants over structures and roles would have to be made on an ad hoc basis after the first discussion section met, and thereafter revised on a session-by-session basis to allow for changes in attendance. Detailing a member of the research team to do this, moreover, meant another loss in the monitoring process.

The researchers reviewed the rationale behind the design and procedures, telephoned two colleagues for consultation, and finally decided that intermittent, rather than continuous, monitoring of the groups would provide adequate information. The team members could thus be allowed to float from one group to another, thereby freeing several people to make assign-

172

ments and covering for the one who was sick. Because they knew that some discussants would finish before others, however, and that some would immediately go on to their new assignments while others would linger in conversation, get lost trying to find their next location, or slip off to do other things between sessions, the team also realized that each one would have to be more active in steering people to their places, picking up and distributing materials, and starting and stopping discussions than they planned when a larger number of researchers were assigned. A supply of hotel plans was obtained, and the team members spent some time marking the location of the meeting rooms clearly on these, to aid the participants in finding their assignments. Late in the evening, the conference organizer stopped by to see how things were going and reminded the researchers that a small group of teenagers from the church youth clubs had volunteered to serve as conference aides. The organizer offered to mobilize them as guides and meeting assistants, who could help to manage the materials during the discussions. The researchers arranged to meet the young people at an early breakfast and to brief them. A number of high school students came to the breakfast and agreed to help, although they would require close supervision at first.

When the participants assembled the next morning, the anticipated difficulties in fact occurred. Delegates and visitors who had not previously registered appeared and asked to join, while many who had been expected to take part decided to do other things. Making up the groups proved to be a slow and inefficient process, with participants unable to understand why they could not be in groups with their friends or work on particular issues they preferred, or had to take assigned roles. The slow sign-up caused delays in starting all the discussions, which by the end of the day were running more than an hour behind, interfering with and being impeded by other planned activities. Necessary changes in the written materials had to be composed on the spot and given to participants, with care taken that the modifications were correctly noted and were included in further procedures. These tasks added to the burdens on the research team, who fell further behind in running the groups according to the design. A number of the participants expressed strong dissatisfaction with the disorganization they experienced, and they decided to leave the experiment, thus compounding the problems of assignment and scheduling. And, most unfortunately, an opinionated and irritated delegate undertook to lecture one of the investigators on how research ought to be done. Harassed, overworked, and himself confused by the situation, the researcher lost his temper, and a loud quarrel quickly involved several participants on either side. Other participants intervened, the researcher apologized, and the discussions continued. The researcher was aware, however, that the argument was likely to have contaminated the group.interactions he was studying and that those groups' products would have to be excluded.

In the event, the confusion caused by making last-minute group assignments and the inadequate control over the discussion groups' progress resulted in the loss of data from a number of the groups. By chance, most of these missing groups happened to be in one of the experimental conditions, so that the entire condition had to be excluded from the analyses. While the results of the study proved to be interesting and suggestive, they failed to provide the complete test of the hypothesis which had been planned.

Which of these problems could have been predicted and alleviated? A number of the difficulties could certainly have been foreseen, and better information would have led to solutions. Very likely the researchers had never attended church conventions, but some of them, at least, had taken part in other meetings. They should certainly have been aware that large meetings seldom start exactly on time and that delegates frequently do other things during conventions besides attend formal sessions. Enough flexibility should have been built into the schedule to allow for the member who stops in the doorway of the meeting room to chat with old friends, or the effects of jet lag which cause travelers to oversleep in the morning or crave a nap after lunch. It would have been wise to check with the conference officials on how many visitors would attend, in addition to the registered participants. And a colleague who cannot control his temper under the stress of fieldwork would be well advised to limit his scholarly activities to library research.

Certain other problems, however, are hard to predict. Membership on a research team usually does not require a health certificate, although illness can seriously disrupt the conduct of the study. Planning fieldwork, however, should include some acknowledgment that the work of team members may be lost, and a small surplus of person/hours should be included. How large this surplus should be depends on such factors as the cost of training and supplying that person, as against the harm which his or her absence might do. Telephoning to summon an extra graduate student from the department to help out at the research site a few blocks away costs little. Paying the air fare, hotel bills, and salary of an additional staff member on the other side of the continent might not be warranted, depending on the project. An occasion for research which occurs only once should not be jeopardized to save money or time.

A well-planned study, then, includes planning for contingencies which should not occur. Estimates of the amount of resources allocated to a backup reserve can be made in a number of ways. While published research rarely describes the things that went wrong with the project, informal conversations with researchers can elicit spine-tingling reminiscences of near disasters averted, or almost averted. Failing such sources of information, it would be useful for the project directors to think back over their own memories of complex operations they have engaged in, such as weddings or family vacations. An objective review of such activities will usually single out the problems and critical points where things did not go according to plan. Remembering the anxieties of those times, and how they were dealt with, can prepare the researchers for similar tests.

Conducting fieldwork successfully does not demand that

175

no problems occur. Rather, it requires that the investigators recognize the probability of meeting difficulties and equip themselves physically and mentally to cope with them. The value of research conducted in real-life settings is sufficiently high to make the efforts involved worthwhile. Attention to the logistics of the situation can make even intensive efforts manageable and rewarding.

Selected Readings

--------◆◆-◆◆-◆◆-◆◆-◆◆-◆◆-◆◆-◆◆-◆◆-◆◆-◆◆-◆◆-◆◆--------

Literature on field research, for the most part, has centered on its more academic aspects. Although there are rich resources on research design and analysis applicable to work in the field, relatively little has appeared that treats the mundane questions of practical management. A Venetian diplomat at the court of Louis XIV, when enjoined to marvel at the wonders of nature, is alleged to have replied, "I see no wonder in these gardens equal to seeing myself in them." In a similar vein, writers on field research have understandably focused their attention on the investigator in the field. A number of excellent introspective accounts of field studies have described and analyzed the culture shock that the researcher

177

experiences; the subtle adaptations required as the investigators explore, test, and finally accept their roles; and the initial and continuing interactions between researcher and subject. Such approaches exemplify real concern for the integrity, psychological well-being, and ethical standards of the researchers and, by extension, of their subjects; but they neglect equally important problems of procedure and operation. Nevertheless, a number of writers have addressed the practical issues of managing field-work, either specifically or in the context of a particular research project. These references can be found in many disciplines—and also in fiction. The best ones provide both clear details of technical operations and a sensitive recounting of what actually happens in the field. For a number of reasons having to do with commercial applications, scale, and participation by political and business organizations, the literature is disproportionately directed toward the conduct of survey research. The techniques and logic of surveys and other types of field investigations, however, are sufficiently similar so that the sources can be informative and helpful regardless of the specific data-collecting mechanism utilized. Since the prototype of a field operation is seen in military campaigns, several references deal with military and quasi-military action.

The following publications are grouped under headings that parallel the chapter titles of this book. In many cases, however, the fit is loose, and many of the readings are applicable to—and some are listed under—more than one heading.

Planning for Field Operations*

Cook, T. D., and Campbell, D. T. "The Design and Conduct of Quasi-Experiments and True Experiments in Field Settings." In M. E. Dunnette (Ed.), *Handbook of Industrial and Organizational Psychology.* Chicago: Rand McNally,

*Publications listed in this section also include general considerations of the researcher's role and the design of fieldwork.

Selected Readings

1976. See, in particular, the sections on "Conduct of True Experiments" and "Situations Conducive to Field Experiments" for discussions of adaptation of research methodology to field situations.

Junker, B. H. *Field Work: An Introduction to the Social Sciences.* Chicago: University of Chicago Press, 1960. Focuses on questions of the researcher's role and relationships, but also provides telling vignettes of field operations.

Michener, J. "Alligator." In *Tales of the South Pacific.* New York: Macmillan, 1946. A fictionalized account of the organization of a military operation, which demonstrates large-scale planning processes for field activities.

Orne, M. T. "On the Social Psychology of the Psychological Experiment: With Particular Reference to Demand Characteristics and Their Implications." *American Psychologist,* 1962, *17,* 776-783. A discussion of subject and interviewer expectations, with emphasis on methods of protecting validity.

Schatzman, L., and Strauss, A. L. *Field Research: Strategies for a Natural Sociology.* Englewood Cliffs, New Jersey: Prentice-Hall, 1973. Presentation of strategies for entering into and maintaining research relationships, with emphasis on the effect of fieldwork interactions on the perspective of the researcher.

Wax, R. *Doing Fieldwork.* Chicago: University of Chicago Press, 1971. An account of fieldwork under conditions of societal stress, with discussions of the benefits and dangers of investigator acculturation and participation. There are especially valuable notes on the researcher as a tool of the subject and on techniques for maintaining objectivity and a distance that permits reliable observation.

179

Selected Readings

Webb, E. J., and others. *Unobtrusive Measures: Nonreactive Research in the Social Sciences.* Chicago: Rand McNally, 1966. Utilization of physical, archival, and observational sources of data; see especially the chapters on natural versus contrived settings and on open versus surreptitious observation.

Weick, K. L. "Systematic Observational Methods." In G. Lindzey and E. Aronson, *Handbook of Social Psychology.* Vol. 2. (2nd ed.) Reading, Mass.: Addison-Wesley, 1968. Distinguishes between natural and evoked behaviors and explains how the research setting can facilitate recognition and recording of verbal and behavioral responses.

Wright, C. R., and Hyman, H. H. "The Evaluators." In P. E. Hammond (Ed.), *Sociologists at Work.* New York: Basic Books, 1964. A description of collaborative research, including the development of detailed work schedules.

Research Sites and Settings

Humphrey, L. *Tearoom Trade: Impersonal Sex in Public Places.* Chicago: Aldine, 1970. Discusses the problems and solutions required in setting up and conducting research under adverse conditions in public park restrooms.

Johnson, W. T. "Researching the Religious Crusade: A Personal Journal." In M. P. Golden (Ed.), *The Research Experience.* Itasca, Ill.: Peacock, 1976. Describes in detail the procedures for establishing and maintaining work in a field location.

Weinberg, E. *Community Surveys with Local Talent.* Chicago: National Opinion Research Center, 1971. Suggestions on setting up a local office in the community under study.

Selected Readings

Whyte, W. F. *Street Corner Society.* Chicago: University of Chicago Press, 1955. See, in particular, the appendix, in which the author describes his living conditions during the course of the study.

Communications, Information, and Authorization

Backstrom, C. H., and Hursh, G. D. *Survey Research.* Evanston, Ill.: Northwestern University Press, 1963. Primarily concerned with the conduct of political opinion surveys; includes sections on public information dissemination and public relations.

Brandt, R. M. *Studying Behavior in Natural Settings.* New York: Holt, Rinehart and Winston, 1972. Emphasis on research in schools, with discussions on gaining acceptance and building rapport.

Festinger, L., Riecken, H. W., and Schacter, S. *When Prophecy Fails.* Minneapolis: University of Minnesota Press, 1956. A classic account of research with members of a quasi-religious community; details the processes of communication within and about the conduct of the study.

Lurie, A. *Imaginary Friends.* New York: Coward, McCann & Geoghegan, 1967. A fictionalized account of a study that appears essentially similar to that reported by Festinger; accentuates the personal relationships and interactions between members of the research team and the subjects.

Staffing the Project

Chapin, F. S. *Field Work and Social Research.* New York: Appleton-Century-Crofts, 1920. An example of the recurring nature of field personnel problems; Chapin's sugges-

Selected Readings

tions on recruiting and selecting field staff are as applicable today as they presumably were fifty years ago.

Kinsey, A. C. *Sexual Behavior in the Human Male.* Philadelphia: Saunders, 1948. Chap. 2, which describes the specifications and selection criteria for interviewers, is a model for these activities.

U.S. Bureau of the Census. No single manual for the selection of field staff has been developed, but materials are prepared for each census project, providing basic criteria and selection procedures. Copies of the various study manuals are available for reference from regional offices.

Field Staff Management

Converse, J., and Schuman, H. *Conversations at Random: Survey Research as Interviewers See It.* New York: Wiley, 1974. Examples of management information and communications to and from the field, including vivid anecdotes. An excellent introduction to the realities of conducting fieldwork at long distance.

Riesman, D., and Watson, J. "The Sociability Project: A Chronicle of Frustration and Achievement." In P. E. Hammond (Ed.), *Sociologists at Work.* New York: Basic Books, 1964. See especially the section on "The Organization and Disorganization of Work," which details the problems of managing an ongoing project.

U.S. Bureau of the Census. Operations manuals for specific studies, as described under the previous heading.

Weinberg, E. *Community Surveys with Local Talent.* Chicago: National Opinion Research Center, 1971. Specific techniques for managing an inexperienced staff, with particular attention to issues of housing and pay for lower socioeconomic status staff members. Includes examples of quality control and management forms.

Cost Estimates, Budgeting, and Money Management

Davis, J. A. "Great Books and Small Groups: An Informal History of a National Survey." In P. E. Hammond (Ed.), *Sociologists at Work.* New York: Basic Books, 1964. In part, describes the initiation of a naive researcher into the financial realities of conducting research.

Jones, S. B. "Personal Reflections on the Research in Process." In M. P. Golden (Ed.), *The Research Experience.* Itasca, Ill.: Peacock, 1976. Another account of a researcher coping with the tangled finances of field research.

Sudman, S. *Reducing the Cost of Surveys.* NORC Monographs. Chicago: Aldine, 1967. Reports the results of research on increasing efficiency and reducing field costs of survey research; includes copies of management forms.

Webb, K., and Hatry, H. *Obtaining Citizen Feedback: Application of Citizen Surveys to Local Government.* Washington, D.C.: Urban Institute, 1973. Examples of costing various elements of fieldwork.

Materials, Supplies, and Suppliers

Coyle, J. J., and Bardi, E. J. *Management of Business Logistics.* St. Paul, Minn.: West Publishing, 1976. One of a number of books in the relatively new field of distribution management. Oriented toward business, but also presents an elementary view of the subject useful to researchers in other disciplines.

Forsyth, F. *Dogs of War.* New York: Viking Press, 1974. Procurement of materials in a quasi-military operation.

Selected Readings

U.S. Army. Army Regulations: AR 710-2—*Inventory Management* and AR 735-5—*Property Accountability: General Principles, Policies, and General Procedures.* Used in logistics training, these manuals offer a general overview of supply management techniques.

Documentation

Humphrey, L. *Tearoom Trade: Impersonal Sex in Public Places.* Chicago: Aldine, 1970. Sections of the book describe procedures for securing and handling records containing extremely sensitive personal data.

Parten, M. *Surveys, Polls, and Samples: Practical Procedures.* New York: Cooper Square, 1966. A section on the preparation and publication of reports provides detailed information on format and content.

Schatzman, L., and Strauss, A. L. *Field Research Strategies for a Natural Sociology.* Englewood Cliffs, New Jersey: Prentice-Hall, 1973. Chapter 6, "Strategy for Recording," offers valuable hints on primary handling of notes and records.

Selltiz, C., Wrightsman, L., and Cook, S. W. *Research Methods in Social Relations.* (3rd ed.) New York: Holt, Rinehart and Winston, 1976. Chap. 15 presents guidelines for report writing.

Sudman, S. *Reducing the Cost of Surveys.* NORC Monographs. Chicago: Aldine, 1967. Use of management records for accounting and reporting.

U.S. Army. Army Regulations: AR 340-2—*Maintenance and Disposition of Records.*

Selected Readings

Managing Field Operations

Several of the readings cited appear in *The Research Experience,* edited by M. Patricia Golden. This book, which follows each research report with a personal memoir by the researcher on his or her experiences in the field, is probably the best current presentation of how field research is done and what it does to its practitioners. *The Research Experience* is recommended as a general reference to introduce field research in all its complexity to novices—and to reinforce the teachings of experience to the rest of us.

Index

186

Index

187

Index

Parten, M., 184
Planning: documentation of, 142-146; example of, 16-17; operations schedule for, 6-11; process of, 1-17; time concepts for, 11-13

Reports, as documentation, 149-151
Researcher, individual: and authorization, 43; and documentation, 150; and money management, 110-111, 114; and planning, 2-3
Riecken, H. W., 181
Riesman, D., 182

Schacter, S., 181
Schatzman, L., 179
Schedule, operations. *See* Operations schedule
Schuman, H., 182
Selltiz, C., 184
Sherif, C. W., 3-4
Sherif, M., 3-5
Sites and settings: adaptation and utilization of, 24-28; authorization for, 19-24; examples of, 21-22, 25-26, 29-34, 35-37; for field headquarters, 34-37; management of people at, 27-28; permission from users of, 20-24; selection of independent, 28-34; walk through of, 31-34
Sponsorship: and authorization, 40-43; and donated staff, 71-72
Staff: advertising for, 75-76; calculation of person/hours needed for, 54-63; donated by sponsor, 71-72; examples of management of, 54-62, 65-67, 68-70, 73-74, 77-79, 91-92; factors in selection of, 65-67; of friends and relatives, 90-92; hiring of, 82-85; interactions of, monitored, 165-167; management of, 81-103; objectiv-

ity of, 72-75; pay of and working conditions for, 85-88; qualifications for, 63-65; recruiting methods for, 75-80; recruitment and selection of, 53-80; safety of, 161-165; screening applications for, 77-80; sources of, 67-72; subcontracting of, 102-103; supervision of, 88-90; training of, 92-102; volunteers as, 83-84, 90-92; written details for, 84-85
Strauss, A. L., 179
Sudman, S., 183, 184
Supervision, of staff, 88-90
Supplies. *See* Materials and supplies

Time: concepts of, in planning, 11-13; and delays and down time, 15-17; duration of, 12-13; and flexibility, 13-14, 16-17; and occurrence, 11-12
Timelines, as documentation, 144, 145-146
Training: agenda for, 97-101; materials for, 93, 95-97; of staff, 92-102

U.S. Army, 184
U.S. Bureau of the Census, 182

Volunteers, as staff, 83-84, 90-92

Walk through: for management, 159; for materials and supplies, 126; of sites and settings, 31-34
Watson, J., 182
Wax, R., 179
Webb, E. B., 180
Webb, K., 183
Weick, K. L., 180
Weinberg, E., 180, 182
Whyte, W. F., 181
Wright, C. R., 180
Wrightsman, L., 184

DATE DUE